MYSTE

RELIGION

Newman's Epistemology of Religion

Clyde Nabe
Southern Illinois University

UNIVERSITY
PRESS OF
AMERICA

Lanham • New York • London

Copyright © 1988 by

University Press of America,® Inc.

4720 Boston Way
Lanham, MD 20706

3 Henrietta Street
London WC2E 8LU England

Printed in the United States of America

British Cataloging in Publication Information Available

Library of Congress Cataloging-in-Publication Data

Nabe, Clyde, 1940-
Mystery and religion : Newman's epistemology of religion / Clyde
Nabe.
p.   cm.
Includes index.
1. Newman, John Henry, 1801-1890—Contributions in doctrine of
faith and reason.   2. Newman, John Henry, 1801-1890—Contributions
in theory of knowledge in religion.   3. Faith and reason—History of
doctrines—19th century.   4. Knowledge, Theory of (Religion)—
History of doctrines—19th century.   I. Title.
BT50.N483N33   1988
231'.042'0924—dc19   87-27472 CIP
ISBN 0-8191-6711-8 (alk. paper)
ISBN 0-8191-6712-6 (pbk. : alk. paper)

All University Press of America books are produced on acid-free
paper which exceeds the minimum standards set by the National
Historical Publications and Records Commission.

Dedication: To Frederick Ferre, who allowed this
   journey to begin

ACKNOWLEDGEMENTS: To Southern Illinois University, the
    School of Humanities, and the Department of Philosophical
    Studies who allowed me a sabbatical leave so that I could
    have the time to do the research and reflection necessary
    for this work to be done; to Galen Pletcher who encouraged
    and urged this work to be completed; and to Donna Stubble-
    field, whose patience allowed me to learn to work with
    a computer--many, many grateful thanks.

From a GRAMMAR OF ASSENT: An Essay in Aid of, by John Henry
    Newman, intro. by Nicholas Lash. c. 1979 by University
    of Notre Dame Press. Reprinted by permission.

From NEWMAN'S UNIVERSITY SERMONS, by John Henry Newman. c. 1970
    by SPCK. Reprinted by permission.

INTRODUCTION

John Henry Newman was deeply concerned throughout his life about the relationships between religious faith and human reason. From the University Sermons, preached to the Oxford community in the 1830s to his Essay in Aid of a Grammar of Assent written in 1870, epistemological questions provide a thread of continuity throughout the development of Newman's thinking. Newman was uncomfortable with the exaggerated claims made by some of his contemporaries about the reliability of human reason. He sought to show that faith does not arise from reason, but rather more often than not precedes its ruminations. Newman believed that reason could support faith; it could be, and indeed ought to be used to test faith claims. But it could not demonstrate faith to be in error; nor could it exhaustively explain or make sense of faith. Faith exceeded the ability of reason to comprehend it. Religious faith was too great for human reason to encompass; it was too big a bite for reason to digest.

This viewpoint has a long history in Western thought. In the fourth century an African bishop of the Christian church wrote "it is rational that faith precedes reason in the case of certain great matters...[1]" Three quarters of a millenium later, an English bishop of that same church (Anselm) prefaced one of his arguments purportedly demonstrating the existence of God with a paraphrase of Augustine's dictum: "I do not seek to understand that I may believe, but I believe in order to understand[2]." The works of these theologians suggest then that understanding religious truth (or rather some religious truths) can only occur in a context of religious faith. At least on some matters one must begin with faith; understanding must follow later.

The qualification in the quotation above from Augustine's work ("in the case of certain great matters") is significant, and is reflected in what I have just written. Newman too believed that faith precedes reason, particularly in certain matters.

Specifically, Newman held that in matters of what he called <u>moral</u> concern (i.e., in concrete matters, or matters of <u>action</u>), faith takes precedence. This point will be elucidated below.

But to understand Newman fully on these matters, we must also note that on his view what has been said so far about "reason" is too vague. That is, Newman would agree with what has been stated here (and below) if one makes plain what is meant by the term "reason". Newman believed that human rationality is a richer phenomenon than what many philosophers and theologians refer to when they discuss "reason." This issue too will be dealt with extensively in the following chapters.

Newman thus shared with Augustine and Anselm a distrust of another view of the relationship between faith and reason. That view emphasizes that the final arbiter in all cases must be reason. If faith produces a claim which is unacceptable at the bar of reason, that claim must be rejected. This view can lead to the position that philosophy and theology, or science and religion, are at war with each other. David Hume's empiricist epistemology and W. K. Clifford's exaggerated claims about the morality of reason come to mind here. To such thinkers, faith follows upon, or should follow upon, or even from, the successful conclusion of an argument. Religious belief on this second view arises in a context of human rationalilty and finds its (only) justification in that source. I believe that this view is the prevalent one in most twentieth century Western minds. It began to become the dominant view in sixteenth and seventeenth century Europe. Descartes, Spinoza, and Leibniz on the continent; Hobbes, Locke, and Hume in England; these thinkers solidified the attitude that human reason must be the measure of all truth. What could not be measured by reason was held to be incapable of being accepted--and thus, incapable of being (appropriately) believed.

So to a mentality coming to maturity and educated in the rational empiricistic culture of the twentieth century Newman's claims are profoundly controversial. The twentieth century Western mind is one formed by Baconian and Cartesian rational modes of thought. To this mentality what can not be made to fit the standards of reason must be consigned to darkness. Or as Wittgenstein put it in the <u>Tractatus:</u> "what we cannot speak about we must pass over in silence[3]." Positivism may be officially out of favor in philosophical circles. But it (or one of its incarnations) is alive and well in the scientific community, in much of the educational system, and even unofficially in much philosophical thought of this period. Thus Newman's work has not been successful if its aim was to undercut the domination of an overrationalized mentality.

But Newman's way of thinking is of interest today because we seriously question the great trust in the capacity of human reason eventually to know all. The limitations of human reason in allowing our world to stand before us in clarity have become even more obvious than they were in Newman's time. These limitations are not merely quantitative ones; it is not just that human reason is not large enough or developed enough to see all. Instead there are inherent limitations to this way of meeting our reality. This has become clear in science itself, most notably in mathematics and physics. (Think here of Heisenberg's Uncertainty Theory, and of Godel's theorem in mathematics.)

Thus when Newman railed against the "liberals" at Oxford, he was arguing for a view to which the twentieth century is slowly being forced to accede. Human reason is not boundless in its capacity to bring us to truth; in fact, there are truths and aspects of reality which persistently evade reason's searchlight.

One response to this is to argue that where human reason can not bring something to light, one must remain agnostic-- unknowing. Newman was uncomfortable with that claim. He believed that the shadows could often be penetrated by the human mind; even when reason could not perform such investigations exhaustively, we can come to some understanding.

The intention here is carefully to examine Newman's work to make plain what he saw to be human ways to truth. Since Newman was particularly concerned with religious faith and truth, we will follow his lead. Indeed our work here will be concerned to show that much religious truth evades the limits of human reason. Our investigations will in each case involve paying close attention to Newman's views on the matter at hand. Launching from that shore, we will seek to show how Newman's views and insights can help us here late in the twentieth century better to understand how religious assertions can be evaluated.

Newman stands in a tradition which argues that religious assertions are justifiable in a particular way: probability. Joseph Butler in the eighteenth century used a similar claim to argue against the hyperrational Deists, and Newman claimed to be influenced in his thinking by Butler. Thus Newman in the nineteenth century reiterated and developed Butler's views. Those views have arisen again in the twentieth century: Basil Mitchell has argued that probability is a way to support religious assertions, as has Richard Swinburne[4]. A line of argument which reappears again and again historically is one which bears examination for it appeals to reflective minds in different historico-cultural milieux.

We will focus on Newman because his arguments seem to me to be some of the best statements of the view that probability is the way of religious life. Writing in a period when British intellectual life was becoming ever more dominated by empiricist scientific modes of thinking, Newman clearly recognized what that domination portended for human life. His insights into the limits of such thinking are vigorous; his arguments about its limitations are persuasive. He will be an excellent guide for us.

NOTES

1. Saint Augustine's Epist. 120, P.L. xxxiii.453, quoted in
   St. Anselm's Proslogion, translated by M. J. Charlesworth
   (London: Oxford University Press, 1965), 27.

2. Saint Anselm. Basic Writings, translated by S. N. Deane
   (LaSalle, Illinois: Open Court Publishing Company,
   1968), 7.

3. Wittgenstein, Ludwig. Tractatus Logico-Philosophicus
   (London: Routledge & Kegan Paul, 1961), Section 7.

4. Mitchell, Basil, The Justification of Religious Belief
   (New York: Oxford University Press, 1981); Swinburne,
   Richard, The Existence of God (Oxford: Clarendon
   Press, 1979).

Chapter 1

I

John Henry Newman is notorious in some circles for having argued that religion needs to be <u>more</u> supernatural, not less. The rationalist finds such an argument threatening. That assertion is open to undesirable interpretations, for it seems to be an appeal to obscurantism. Newman also often claimed that religion inevitably involved mystery. Again, "mystery" and "mysteriousness" make believers in human reason alone uncomfortable.

This essay will concern itself with "mystery" and its possible proper place in thought about religion. We will examine how Newman used this term, and seek out any differences there might be between mystery and obscurantism. My contention will be that Newman nowhere appeals to mystery-making in order to obfuscate a matter; rather he saw a clear distinction to be drawn between fuzzy-minded thinking and genuine mystery. I will also show that when Newman claims that there is a place for the supernatural in religion he means that religion goes <u>beyond</u> the natural, and in particular beyond "natural reason." Thus this essay will also involve itself in a careful examination of Newman's understanding of human reason. By studying the extent to which he found human reason limited, and the distinctions he made between different uses of reason, we will be able to come to better grips with his use of "mystery."

This is productive work for us today because Newman's contributions to the understanding of human intelligence and how we come to know are important ones. Newman was not a systematic philosopher; his attempts at philosophical understanding arise in the contexts of particular questions about religious faith. So no developed method is to be found in his work. What is of interest to us is his philosophical response to the intellectual developments of his time, and to the claims about the rationality of religious belief which came out of those intellectual developments. Similar claims are made today, except that over a century such claims have developed, become stronger, and become the pervasive attitude of our century. Newman early saw the force of those claims and attempted to show that they were based on no necessary truths about the nature of human knowledge. Indeed, he would argue that the assumptions of those he called "liberal" thinkers (and who I will call "rationalists") were in error. They were in error precisely because they had too narrow a view of human reason, and of how human reason properly operates.

We will begin then with Newman's analysis of human reason. When we are clearer about that, we will be in a good position to understand his view of the role of mystery in discussions of religion.

II

Newman worked on his understanding of human reason throughout his life. One place in which we can find long discussions of his thinking about this topic is in his University Sermons. These came relatively early in his career (in 1826-1843, as opposed to the Essay in Aid of a Grammar of Assent, which is perhaps his major single attempt to grapple with this problem, and which was published in 1870). Of course as sermons they are not developed at as much length or in as much depth as one would expect in essays meant to be published. Still they are in some ways as clear statements of Newman's position as can be found. We begin then by looking at what he says in them about human reason.

At the very beginning of this series, in a sermon preached in 1826, Newman argued that religion is not opposed to reason. Indeed

> the whole Bible...tells us that truth is too sacred and religious a thing to be sacrificed to the mere gratification of the fancy, or amusement of the mind, or party spirit, or the prejudices of education, or attachment...to the opinions of human teachers, or any...other feelings...[1]

Rejecting all of those as appropriate sources alone of faith, Newman pointed to an important connection between reason and faith. He was not interested in divorcing the two. MacKinnon is correct then in arguing that Newman is not a supporter of those who see faith as "a leap in the dark.[2]" Throughout his life Newman held this view that reason and faith are in a vital relationship to each other. In 1840 he would argue that faith is

2

in all cases a reasonable process [3]; and in the <u>Grammar</u> he would urge that "in religion the imagination and affections should always be under the control of reason[4]."

If Newman saw reason as important to discussions of religious faith, it might seem surprising that he also strongly attacked reason in this matter. Newman built much of his intellectual life around a negative response to the rationalism he found at Oxford. Indeed one of his major works, the apologetic of the <u>Apologia</u>, centers on a controversy with Charles Kingsley about Newman's supposed subversion of reason in matters of religious belief. How is this to be made sense of in terms of our earlier claim that Newman is not an anti-rationalist in his religious epistemology? The answer lies in that for Newman there is reason, and then there is reason. This is seen most clearly when we study his university sermon of 1840 entitled "Implicit and explicit reason."

Newman believed that epistemologists had not paid close enough attention to the way in which reason is present in human life. Being human in Newman's eyes meant to operate in the world as a reasoning creature, but it meant this <u>among other things</u>. That is, Newman did not equate being human merely with being one who reasons; thus he proclaimed exaggeratedly, "man is <u>not</u> a reasoning animal; he is a seeing, feeling, contemplating, acting animal.[5]" So reason does make a human being human, but it <u>alone</u> does not accomplish this. We see that in his anthropology, as in other areas of his thought, Newman first of all combatted an over-emphasis on rationality. On Newman's view, such an over-emphasis developed out of a misunderstanding of human reason, and a myopia about how it fit into the complexity of human life and experience.

He believed that when we give careful reflection to reason's presence in our lives we discover that there is a two-levelled (that is, <u>at least</u> two-levelled) operation of reason in ourselves. Everyone uses the first level; not all are able to operate, in all matters, at the second level.

The first level of human rationality, or perhaps better, the first way in which human reason operates was termed "implicit reason" by Newman in his university sermon. There he first of all identified reason as "a living, spontaneous energy within us, not an art.[6]" Even at this level, reason is a faculty for gaining knowledge. Such a gain may occur without direct perception, and involves discovering something by means of something else. This sounds vague of course, and it is. But such vagueness was inevitable in Newman's eyes. He believed that reason as it operates in everyday life does not operate with full clarity. Descartes' clear and distinct ideas are not discoverable here, at least not very often. Again, he suggests that this level is a level of "unconscious" reasoning.

This sort of language may make us uncomfortable. "Unconscious" and "reasoning" may sound utterly contradictory. Reason is often seen as something that goes on in the full light of consciousness. If there is activity going on outside of consciousness, that activity is precisely what we mean by the "ir-rational" or "non-rational," at least on one view.

But this discomfort begins to lead us in the direction we must go if we are to understand what Newman tried to do. He sought to broaden or deepen our vision of what reasoning involves.

When Newman talked about implicit or unconscious reasoning he was striving to dissociate "reasonable" from "reflective" and "methodologically clear." To be reasonable in everyday life is to have a reason, not necessarily to be able to give a reason[7]. Reasonableness at the implicit level involves an integration of experience, a glimpse of what holds reality together, a perhaps inchoate sense 1) that this makes sense and 2) of how this makes sense. It is to be active in the world with an attitude and perhaps an insight that reality is not incoherent. It is to suspect that behind apparent chaos there is really a cosmos.

The success or failure of Newman's argument here lies, to begin with, in his ability to convince us that 1) implicit reason is a coherent concept, and 2) that it reflects something really operable in human experience.

One way of understanding what Newman is claiming is to think of implicit or unconscious reasoning as being designations of how human beings are in the world. We seek out connections in our experience; our thinking leads us from one thing to another and not in purely random ways. Walking along the seashore, as we watch the waves grow higher and more white-capped, and as we hear them pound onto the sand, and feel them climb ever higher on our legs, we think "The sea is angry." Such ties between different parts of our experience (e.g., the appearance of the ocean and our emotions) go on in us constantly. Those often subconscious trains of thought are essential features of the way in which human beings live into their world. Such trains of thought then are found in our experience; Newman has caught hold of part of our human reality.

But is it coherent to call such trains of thought "reasoning?" Some might urge that they are random, incoherent, irrational. Still, the twentieth century is even more alert to the rarity of "random trains of thought" in human experience than was Newman's own. Already in the nineteenth century there was a growing awareness that there is an unconscious element in human thinking. Goethe, Fichte, and the Romantics all pointed in this direction. We who live after the investigations of psychoanalysts like Freud and Jung are even more aware that seldom are we able to find chains of thinking which are "unconnected." For instance, we have seen that word association tests show that stimuli which come to our minds get associated in recognizable ways with our responses. Sheer randomness in thinking--whatever that would mean--is difficult to discover.

So Newman's view that there is an underlying pattern of reason in human thought and experience seems to be correct, and comprehensible. To get this affirmative result we have to think of reasoning in a very broad sense to be sure. We must see it as little more than trains of thought, unrandom connections of some sort between our ideas.

J. Artz in writing about Newman's view of reason said:

> Before I am able to formulate arguments, I have reasoned spontaneously without being fully conscious of the individual elements or steps. I have surveyed connections, reasons without being able to seize them by my consciousness. Sometimes I am not at all able to formulate them even afterwards, because they are too subtle or too cumulative, too rarefied, or because they have too many implications [8].

This passage brings forth the distinction Newman drew between implicit and explicit reason. Implicit reason is broader and deeper than explicit reason. It comes before, I believe both logically and at least often temporally, explicit reason. Explicit reason involves argument; implicit reason does not. Implicit reason does not go on in the full light of consciousness as I noted earlier, although here it is worth noting that Artz's way of putting this raises a new question. "I have surveyed connections...without being able to seize them them by my consciousness." Who then is the reasoner here? If Artz is correct in his understanding of Newman, and I believe that he is, then it is clear that Newman did not equate the reasoner with the consciousness of the individual. Indeed, Newman wrote again and again that the reasoner in this sense of reason (i.e., implicit reason) is the whole person. He meant by this that when we reason implicitly, we bring into play our sense, feelings, intuition, our heart and mind and soul.

Graham Shute[9] has suggested that there is a similarity between Newman's implicit reason and Pascal's _logique du coeur_. In a famous passage Pascal wrote "The heart has its reasons which reason does not know.[10]" And Pascal argued that mathematical reason (which is one form of reason) has a logic of its own, while the heart also has a logic, which is not the same as the logic of reason. This is the distinction to which Shute is pointing.

Pascal's distinction, however, puts the logique du coeur next to mathematical logic. Newman does not put implicit reason alongside of explicit reason. Rather explicit reason is of a different order or level as I have called it. What is reasoned about is the source of Newman's distinction, not just the method used. Explicit reason is a step back from the reasoning about a particular lived question. It reasons about and reflects upon the activity of implicit reason itself. We see this in the old philosophical saw that human beings not only know, but know that they know. The first phrase might be said to refer to the level of implicit reason. The latter phrase could be seen to mark the level of explicit reason. Explicit reason then is our thinking about our thinking.

But this way of drawing out the differences is not Pascal's. What Shute does have hold of is that for Newman, as for Pascal, mathematical logic is not the only way to knowledge. I think it is more correct to identify Pascal's mathematical logic with Newman's explicit reason than it is to identify Newman's implicit reason with Pascal's logique du coeur. I labor this point a bit to draw attention in another way to what Newman sought to do, i.e., to broaden our notion of reason. In doing this he also tried to show that reason begins or has its source in a human activity which is more ordinary, more everyday, more mundane than the rationalist notices. Descartes' view of reason, and the nineteenth century empiricists' view of it were too refined. They identified reason with reflection on our thinking, i.e., with explicit reason. But Newman did not argue that there is a second way to reason alongside of this, as perhaps Pascal claimed. Newman urged that normal everyday reasoning is the foundation of all reasoning. Explicit reason would not exist were there no first level implicit reasoning going on. Implicit reason is a vast, often murky pool of thinkings about; explicit reason is a step out of that murky pool to examine those thinkings about. Explicit reason then may be seen as a sort of distillation of implicit reason. But, and this was the crucial point for Newman, the process of implicit reasoning is complete in itself, and is independent of any subsequent reflection on it[11].

As I said earlier, epistemological problems interested Newman primarily in the context of questions concerning religious belief. What Newman was ultimately interested in achieving by revealing the level of implicit reasoning was the justification of faith in those who have not reflected upon that faith. So, religious belief in the common man was the goad to Newman's reflections on implicit reasoning.

Newman was concerned about those who suggested that no one is entitled to hold a belief, even if it is true, if they do not also have the justification for that true belief. Those who hold this position argue that to believe what is true is not enough; one must also know why or how it is true. Newman realized that many believers could not provide the epistemological justifications for their beliefs. But he did not believe that this meant such believers were being careless in their faith claims, and it certainly did not mean that they had no "right" to their beliefs.

This claim was made explicit by an Englishman in the late nineteenth century. While I found no evidence that Newman ever read his essay, W. K. Clifford's arguments in "The ethics of belief[12]" typify the view Newman tried to combat. Clifford argued that no one is morally entitled under any circumstances to any belief if (s)he does not have sufficient evidence to support that belief. This is a most significant claim, precisely because it implies that those ordinary believers who cannot give a reason for their beliefs are being immoral in holding such beliefs.

On his own ground, someone who argues like Clifford is probably irrefutable. But Newman tried to suggest that this sort of argument is in fact workable only because it interprets "reason" in the way that it does. And Newman suggested that that interpretation is too narrow. Once one understands that "reason" is broader in signification than the Cliffords allow, their arguments are unpersuasive. In other words, Newman attempted to undercut a basic premise in such an argument. He suggested that the understanding shown in these arguments of how human intelligence operates is in error.

III

Having looked at Newman's presentation of the nature of implicit reason, we will now turn to a closer examination of explicit reason. It is at this level that method is both consciously sought after and made explicit. This is important to note because while there well may be method at the level of implicit reason too, we are unaware of it; and certainly at that level we do not focus our attention on method. So in the Grammar Newman argued that in our ordinary reasoning, we "proceed by a sort of instinctive perception...I call it instinctive...because ordinarily, or at least often, it acts by a spontaneous impulse...[13]" Thus "spontaneity" and "method" are terms which offer us preliminary insight into Newman's distinction between implicit and explicit reason. But this pair of terms will not carry us all the way, and it will need careful elaboration.

Suppose that we get up on a cold morning, and the car does not start. Very rapidly we may 1) check to see if the car is in park or neutral, 2) remember that we just filled it with gas last night, 3) wonder if the starter is broken, and 4) conclude that the battery is dead due to the cold. This chain of thoughts is a form of reasoning. It may or may not involve verbal propositions; that is, we may or may not "say" these things to ourselves. It is relatively spontaneous, and in this process of reasoning we do not pause to think about the methodology of appropriate empirical verification at work. I think that this could be seen as an act of implicit reasoning on Newman's view. Many sorts of thoughts may be involved in it: memories, fantasies, feelings, perceptions. All of these work together in a rapid manner to produce the "instinctive perception" that the battery is dead, due to the cold. This chain of reasoning is independent of analyses about the reliability of memory, the ways in which feelings color our reasoning, the accuracy of sense perceptions, the amount of evidence needed fully to justify a conclusion. That is, Newman would argue, and I think correctly, that when we say "Oh, great! The battery's dead!" in this situation we have 1) reasoned, 2) reasoned correctly, and 3) reached an appropriate conclusion. We are then entitled to our proclamation.

Now suppose that we go back inside, call a neighbor to come over with jumper cables, and return to the car. When we lift up the hood, we discover that the battery has been stolen. In reflecting now upon our earlier reasoning, we probably will say that it was in error. This reflection back on and analysis of the earlier implicit reasoning is an act of what Newman calls explicit reasoning. In this analysis, we will say something like "That earlier reasoning was in error because I did not collect enough empirical evidence." So in this sort of reasoning we appeal to a rule or law of reasoning: "To be fully justified, conclusions about causal relationships ought to be supported by sufficient empirical evidence." We have moved away from what we might call existential reasoning, that is, reasoning done in the face of personal lived life, to the _art_ of reasoning.

Notice that one characteristic of this second-order reasoning is that it occurs in the light of consciousness. When we think about our thinking, we are involved in reflection, and reflection requires light. It is also a process which usually requires a good deal more time than does first-order reasoning. This is not an invariable characteristic, but it is rare for second-order reason to operate in a "spontaneous" manner. In part this is due to the fact that this level of rationality deliberately searches out rules, and seeks meticulously to follow them.

Those rules are finally logical rules. Such rules try to elucidate the form of proper reasoning, and that form is argument. At this level, method, proof, demonstration, and argument are important contents of the reasoning going on. In explicit reason we see that what is being reasoned about need not influence our analysis of the form which that reasoning has taken. So at this level we abstract from the immediate concerns which were the stimulus for the prior act of implicit reasoning. And since immediate, existential concerns are not the focus of attention for explicit reason, the person who performed the earlier acts of implicit reasoning also is not important here.

The paragraph just completed, in which several of Newman's comments about explicit reason are integrated, strikes one also as being at least a preliminary description of what many call "science" or the "scientific method." That method is 1) rule bound, 2) not dependent in its consequence on a particular event, and 3) not dependent in its conclusion on the person doing the reasoning. That is, science is objective.

There have been, of course, innumerable long discussions of the meaning of objectivity in science. To delve deeply into these would lead us too far astray. What is important to us here about this is that Newman saw science and its method as lying at the level of explicit reason. Now Newman probably had too naive a notion of scientific method; his scientific hero par excellence was Newton, and the science which Newman saw as exemplary was mathematics[14]. These models may have led him to make a too tidy distinction between science/explicit reason and implicit reason. Studies in recent philosophy of science have sought to show that 1) being bound to any easily identifiable law of reason or logic, 2) being wholly independent of the subject matter under investigation, and even 3) being unrelated to the person carrying out the study are often too hastily assigned as attributes to "scientific method.[15]"

Rather than being polar opposites, explicit and implicit reason are more likely different regions on the continuum of human rationality. Indeed, we could argue that Newman is too much exercised in drawing his distinction so plainly. Human reason may be seen as less a matter of levels as I have called it, and more as a matter of being now here, now there on the continuum of rationality. Whenever we reason, we do so in the same way. What is implicit or explicit is the method of reasoning. In implicit reasoning that method is not in the spotlight on stage. (It may, however, be in the shadows.) In explicit reasoning it (more or less) is on stage, in the spotlight. We will see later how this modification of Newman's discussion affects our understanding of religious faith.

Another way in which Newman clarified the difference between implicit and explicit reason was to focus attention on the role of language in such reasoning. In the Grammar Newman wrote, 'Verbal reasoning, of whatever kind, as opposed to mental, is what I mean by inference, which differs from logic only inasmuch as logic is its scientific form.[16]" There are three terms here which need careful attention: a) mental reasoning, b) verbal reasoning, and c) logic. First of all, notice that there are three terms, rather than only two as we might expect on the basis of our earlier reflections. In the Grammar Newman recognized three forms of inference: formal, informal, and natural. I have been roughly equating the term "informal inference" which Newman used in the Grammar with the term "implicit reason" which he used in the University Sermons, and similarly "formal inference" with "explicit reason." This identity can be accepted up to a point. In particular, the intersubstitutability of explicit reason and formal inference seems clear. These two, at least at their most formal and most explicit, are also the "logic" to which Newman refers in the passage above. Logic for Newman then is the scientific form of explicit reason or formal inference. Logic is the furthest form of abstraction in human thought. While words or terms are still used in logic, those words or terms have the least amount of concrete content. Algebra, geometry, even Newtonian laws of motion are exemplars of this level of human rationality. Indeed, for Newman this level of extreme abstraction is "Rationality." Rationality in this sense then is one form or one degree of reasonableness. It is not, however, coextensive with reasonableness.

The image Newman has in mind might be represented as follows:

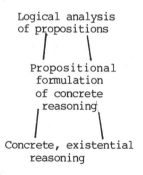

| Logical analysis of propositions | (Empirical effects have empirical causes.) |

| Propositional formulation of concrete reasoning | (When turning the key does not produce ignition, there is something wrong with the electrical system.) |

| Concrete, existential reasoning | (See example above, p. 7) |

The top layer here is the level of logic and of most explicit reason. It is an abstraction from verbal propositions, although it too involves verbal forms. The second level involves the use of language, and so is a level of verbal reasoning as Newman used that term in the passage quoted. For Newman this too, then, is a level of explicit reason. Implicit reason occurs at the level of concrete existential concerns, in one's lived life. At its least verbal and most spontaneous, this is what he calls natural inference. Here there is no formulation of propositions nor any recognition of or movement between premises and conclusion. This is the realm of "mental reasoning" par excellence. And for Newman, one important characteristic of this mental reasoning or natural inference is that the use of language is not involved.

This attempt to uncover language's role in our reasoning again suggests to me that our reasoning is not a matter of kinds or levels, but of a continuum. At one end of that continuum our reasoning is unconscious, preverbal, spontaneous, i.e., here lies natural inference, and our most implicit reason. At the other end, our reasoning is most fully conscious, verbal or even post-verbal, i.e., it involves abstraction from any concrete content in the terms used (twentieth century philosophers would say it uses a meta-language), and is most fully logical, i.e., operating by rules, laws, arguments, proofs. This is our most explicit reason, and our most formal inference. In between there is a mixture of many varied proportions. In between is informal inference, largely verbal reasoning, which varies from being quite explicit to being nearly completely implicit.

This continuum is a better model of human reasoning than Newman's for two reasons: 1) It better reflects our actual experience. Reasoning often has a mixture of verbal components and pre-verbal components. It involves a now largely unconscious use of method and law; now (and sometimes virtually simultaneously) a reflection, however brief, on logical method and rules. We have discovered (in part through the work of the psychoanalysts) how much "pure" logic has unconscious elements at work in it; we have also discovered how much logic there is in our most unconscious mental operations. 2) It allows us to see the same human reason at work everywhere throughout human experience. Newman himself wrote, "We do not reason in one way in chemistry or law, in another in morals or religion...[17]" This is correct; the reason it is correct is that our reasoning is not easily separated into levels, or sorts. Purely spontaneous pre-verbal reasoning, and purely logical, wholly conscious reasoning are limits which help us better to understand how our thinking works. They are not types.

Newman developed his view of the relationship between our reasoning and language in another direction. The inverted funnel appearance of the diagram above is deliberate. Newman held that the more explicit our reasoning becomes, and thus the more verbal, the less it is able to take in all that is going on. Each move toward explicitness and the incarnation of reasoning in language involves a loss of the richness of reasoning itself. So he wrote in the Grammar,

> thought is too keen and manifold, its sources are too remote and hidden, its path too personal, delicate, and circuitous, its subject-matter too various and intricate, to admit of the trammels of any language, of whatever subtlety and of whatever compass.[18]

Anyone who has tried to translate a verbal argument into a symbolical logical form has a good sense of Newman's point here. Words do not easily translate into abstract symbols. Words are too rich, complex, ambiguous. Phrases which include many words are worse on this; propositions of course multiply the problem further. And verbal arguments often prove to be nearly impossible to translate. I remember spending a great deal of time trying to translate what I took to be a relatively simple verbal argument into a symbolical form. After working on it diligently and lengthily I took my translation to a respected logician. He said, "Oh well, one can hardly ever feel confident that a particular translation is adequate or appropriate." I was mightily discouraged. But I was enlightened too. Words into symbols do not go, certainly not easily. Newman's point is that in a similar manner reasoning on a concrete matter also suffers when we try to translate it into words. And he is correct on this.

This has significance for the role of explicit reasoning in our lives. If Newman is correct that "the mind itself is more versatile and vigorous than any of its works, of which language is one,[19]"--and I hold that he is right about this--then language is by its very nature limited in its ability to lay reality open before us. There will be aspects and regions of reality which forever elude language's grasp. And since explicit reason is verbal reasoning, i.e., is dependent upon words for its activity, those aspects and regions of reality also will not be wholly within explicit reason's scope.

And so at last we have arrived at a point where we will be able to explore with greater understanding Newman's use of "super-natural" and "mystery." For Newman these terms apply to that which eludes reason; they are as he termed them above reason. They are not so much outside of reason, as they are too much for reason. Reason can grope toward an understanding of them; it can turn its searchlight into their dark shadows. But the darkness is turbid; the light of reason is not bright enough to penetrate very far into it. It shows up movements, forms and bodies in the darkness, but they are seen so unclearly that what we say about them is bound to be somewhat inaccurate and misleading. So we may now use this word (suffers) and now its apparent contradictory (passionless) for the same subject. In passing, let us note that many who have tried to make clear this difficulty have used a nearly opposite image to the one we just used. That is, they write that that which is above reason is so bright, so fully light that reason's beam is virtually a shaft of darkness. There is good reason to prefer this image in some ways. Reason's beam is so weak compared to that which is being explored that it sometimes actually distorts and makes dark that which it examines. Sometimes any words make things worse; sometimes understanding depends upon our being still, and silencing our reason.

The discussion in the above paragraph must be carefully clarified. Everywhere that one reads the word "reason", one would more appropriately think "explicit reason", "formal inference", "verbal reasoning". To Newman's mind, human reason can always, nay ought always, be in operation. But he means the whole broad range of human reason, not just explicit reason. So, as we noted earlier, he would write, "it is all that I have been saying, that...the imagination and affections should always be under the control of reason"[20]. Thus when he argued that reality eluded reason or was above reason he meant that explicit reason in particular was eluded. Implicit reasoning (and what Reardon in his essay on Newman even more appropriately calls concrete intelligence or concrete reasoning)[21] should always be at work; indeed, I believe that Newman would say nearly always is at work, and correctly so. It can and does lead us in our experience and understanding of reality, including supernatural and mysterious reality.

IV

Reflect for a moment on the following examples:
1) Standing in a cathedral, we look around us in awe. There is the height of the ceiling. It is so far above us that we cannot make out the carvings on its arches. There are the columns on either side of us as we stand in the nave; they stretch upward, and their capitals are lost in the dimness. The arches between them are so numerous and form a pattern so huge that we push our minds as far as they can go to take it in, and still it eludes us. The carvings are so variegated and so profuse that we feel overwhelmed, trying to take them all in. We

strive to make sense of it, to make it into one coherent, simple meaning, but it is too much for us. Our eyes move restlessly from the columns to the carvings to the arches to the mosaics to the windows (blue, red, yellow; human figures, flowers, animals, abstract designs) to the dome. We feel dwarfed, inadequate, unable to grasp it. Our intelligence cannot integrate all this.

2) Or we meet, come to know, and then to love another person. We search that face, those eyes, that bodily form to try to understand what it is that is to us so special about them. We hear that voice in a chorus of voices, and try to discover how it is so unique a production to stand out as it does. We question; we discuss; we spend time with that other person. We come to believe that we know them well; then they escape our knowledge by saying or doing what we would never have predicted that they would say or do. There is ever more to learn, to see, to know of the other.

3) Study any aspect of the world around you carefully. For instance, focus on that which is alive. Begin with some simple description of the biosphere; that which is alive works against the law of entropy. It ingests some energy source from its environment. It excretes matter which is useless to itself or which is used up. It reproduces itself. It arises in time; lives for a certain period; then disappears. This does not go very far toward understanding that which lives. So delve deeper into biology. Every new fact discovered, every new hypothesis confirmed, every new observation leads in the direction of new questions. The living are not grasped by any formulas we propose. They elude our <u>scientia</u>. We are led via our investigations themselves to see that nature is more profound and more difficult to understand than we had believed, or had believed possible.

Using these or similar examples, we learn that our reason, especially our explicit reason, is evaded by reality in all of our life. Our logic and science barely scratch the surface of our everyday experience. Coming up against the limits of that reason is not a rarity; it is the mundane experience of us all. Mystery and that which is above reason are not isolated to the experience of the supernatural (in the pejorative sense of that term). Rather they are commonplace elements which we all run across frequently if not constantly.

When Newman discussed mystery, he was not trying to get us to accept a superstitious obscurantism. In using that term, he was proclaiming that <u>much</u> of our experience is obscure--that is, obscure to explicit reason. Formulas, laws, and simple theories are not able exhaustively to describe nor explain our experience. But this is true throughout our lived experience, not just in some particular part of it. Religious experience is not alone in eluding explicit reason's analysis.

The important point to be made about mystery then is not merely that it exists. That is almost a trivial realization. But Newman's contribution to our philosophy of religion lies on the one hand in his claim that mystery is reasonable, and on the other hand in his attempt to show how reason does illuminate mystery, or that which we see through a glass darkly.

Newman's description of mystery took various forms. In Tract 73, he tied the idea of mystery to "half view and partial knowledge.. guesses, surmises, hopes, and fears...truths faintly apprehended and not understood.[22]" In An Essay on the Development of Christian Doctrine he said that "a mystery implies in part what is incomprehensible or at least unknown...it implies a partial manifestation.[23]"

These statements mix together quite varied acts of human thought. A guess, a hope, and a fear are quite different from truths faintly apprehended. For us the idea of mystery will be associated with terms like the latter, not the former. In fact, Newman himself was more careful about this later. In any case, I intend to see mystery as involving glimpses into reality, with those glimpses leading to some understanding of that reality, but hardly complete understanding. This is where the earlier discussions about explicit reason and implicit reason have led us, and we will follow that lead here.

Mystery then always involves a failure to grasp completely the matter at hand. As I suggested at the beginning of this section, this incompleteness of understanding pervades our intellectual pursuits in all directions. Our knowledge is almost wholly "partial knowledge." Thus mystery is found wherever we turn; it is in particular not isolated in religious experience.

This is not to suggest that all intellectual pursuits are equal in this matter of reality eluding explicit reason. Some disciplines are considerably more successful in getting explicit reason to penetrate the darkness than are others. Modern physical science, mathematics and logic have been remarkably successful in expanding the circle of light around us. One major criterion of that success has been taken to be the ability to manipulate reality, and successfully to exercize power over reality in terms of selected goals. Still, it would be a mistake to see this as the only criterion, or even as the most important criterion in all cases.

In mathematics and logic in particular the degree to which control over reality is a criterion of successful expansion and

clarification of knowledge is small. While new work in these
disciplines may eventually issue in some manipulation of the
world around us, that is not often the goal. And Stephen
Hawkings' attempts to understand black holes and the origin of
the universe do not seem to proceed from an attempt to control
the processes of the universe. My point is that what we choose
as a criterion of the expansion of knowledge should not be too
quickly identified with the Baconian declaration that knowledge
is power. The reason that this is important is that this is a
criticism often leveled at religion (and ethics, aesthetics, and
social science, for that matter). That is, critics often claim
that there has been no increase in our understanding in these
disciplines, because they have not produced new successful
methods of manipulation of reality. But this criticism, even if
it is accurate, does not settle our question of whether or not
there have been increases in our understanding in religion,
morality, and art.

We begin our reflections on this topic then by seeing
mystery as implying partial knowledge. This was how Newman used
the term mystery throughout his reflections. It was in the
Grammar that he most fully discussed what he meant by mystery.
There he clearly related the fact that we are confronted by
mystery to the limitations of our intelligence. So he wrote:
"the words 'mysteriousness' and 'mystery'...are not parts of the
Divine Verity as such, but in relation to creatures and to the
human intellect.[24]" And in his Philosophical Notebook he noted
that he believed that when something was above reason, this arose
from the imperfection of our human intellect[25]. This is what we
would expect given our earlier examination of Newman's view of
human reason. Since he found our explicit reasonings to be
essentially constricted in their ability to manifest the richness
of our experience, it is not surprising that he should find the
murkiness surrounding our understanding of reality to be due to
that constriction.

So it is the nature of the human intellect which brings us
face to face with mystery. Newman went on to explain what
happens in our meeting mystery by exploring the activities of
that intellect. In doing so he began to see mystery as involving
the use of propositions. It is to this analysis we now turn our
attention.

In the Grammar, Newman wrote as follows: "A mystery is a
proposition conveying incompatible notions, or is a statement of
the inconceivable.[26]" To understand his claim here we need to
develop his epistemological language in more depth. The Grammar
is a prolegomenon toward a grammar of assent. Remember that
Newman's goal in this book was to justify the assent to a
religious claim of the person who has a reason for that assent

16

but cannot fully give it. He believed that assent was a mental act which was unconditional. That is, Newman argued that when assent is involved, it is a matter of either yes or no. We do not sort of assent or partially assent or assent more fully now, less fully then. We either assent or we do not. Newman also defined assent as a method of apprehending propositions. To apprehend a proposition meant to Newman to impose a sense on (or to interpret) the terms of which it is composed[27]. Next, he saw propositions as being of different kinds; the most important form of proposition in reference to the mental act of assent is the categorical. A categorical proposition makes an assertion, and implies the absence of any condition or reservation.

In turn, categorical propositions may present to our minds things external to us, or our own thoughts. Facts, causes, effects, actions, qualities: these things Newman called things. In propositions which deal with things like these, the terms are singular terms, for things are units. If the terms in a proposition do not stand for things, then they stand for notions. These terms will be common terms. And as Newman concludes: "Singular (terms) come from experience, common from abstraction.[28]"

This is a somewhat crude epistemology; but then Newman wrote that this was only a beginning. It is true that it is not nearly as easy to distinguish between notions and things as Newman suggests. Nor is the distinction between a common term and a singular term so forthright as Newman might hope. But these problems are not unique to Newman's work. Newman had some familiarity with eighteenth century British empiricist epistemologies, and followed them roughly in this discussion. These epistemologies, while more sophisticated perhaps than Newman's, share some of the same difficulties. In another place in the Grammar Newman argued that apprehensions of things are more forceful than the apprehension of notions[29]. One is strikingly reminded here of Hume's claim in the Treatise and Inquiry that there are two kinds of perceptions: impressions and ideas. Impressions arise from experience; ideas are copies of impressions. And claimed Hume, we can tell an impression from an idea because an impression is more forceful, vivid and lively than an idea. Criticisms leveled at this assertion by Hume seem to be also apposite in reference to Newman's.

All of this is relevant to our concern with Newman's use of mystery because he saw mystery as a disjunction between the notion which we use to stand for a thing, and the thing itself.

We have seen that language is not able to embody reality fully; there is always more to our experience and our reasoning at the implicit level than language allows to be made manifest.

In a similar way, notions fail to embody facts (where "facts" may be seen as events in our experience). Notions are summaries of or distillations of experience. But when we call them distillations, we should not think of them as "purified" facts; they are not essences of our experiences. They are rather less than is really there.

Nevertheless, when we reflect upon our experience, our intellect provides us with notions. In such second order thinking, we are somewhat removed from what is real (the thing). Inevitably then this reasoning suffers from inadequacy. As Newman puts it:

> our notion of a thing may be only partially faithful to the original...it may represent it incompletely...in consequence, it may serve for it...only to a certain point...After that point is reached, the notion and the thing part company...[30]

And there arises the difficulty. When we try to reflect about a thing, we are forced to use notions. That begins our removal to notional propositions. At that point we are using partial copies (to use a Humean term) of the thing, and we are noticing only part of it. If we form another notional proposition of the same thing, we may use notions which in themselves (qua notions) are incompatible with the notions in our first proposition. That is, in reasoning about a tower we may form the proposition "The tower is round," and later we may form the proposition "The tower is square." The notion (tower) in the first proposition is of the tower seen from a distance. The notion (tower) in the second proposition is of the tower seen from closer up. The same tower (thing) is involved, but the notions used to stand for it are different. This analysis leads to a proposition which is an apparent contradiction: "The tower is square and round." But what we really have here are incompatible notions. And so, in Newman's terms, what we have here is a mystery.

We have seen now what Newman means when he says that a mystery is a proposition which conveys incompatible notions. The second approach mentioned in the quotation above was to call a mystery a statement of the inconceivable. This claim proceeds from a different focus by Newman on the nature of mystery.

In this analysis we will have to pay attention to the role of imagination in our reasoning. At least in a preliminary way, Newman saw the imagination as the habit or act of making mental images. In turn, he saw the products of imagination to be made up of conceptions. And conceptions are complex ideas which are consistent in their parts.

We begin then with complex ideas which involve no internal inconsistencies. These can be both conceived and imagined. If these ideas are worked out to their conclusions, no contradictions or paradoxes result. For instance, we can conceive of a deity as being a person like ourselves. Such a deity may be conceived then as experiencing anger, joy, love, envy, etc. Or we may conceive of a deity which is like an Aristotelian unmoved mover. Such a deity will be passionless, and will not experience anger, joy, etc. These conceptions can also be imagined. The first conception of a deity mentioned is easily imagined: think of Zeus or Balder, or the Yahweh of the Torah. Aristotle's unmoved mover is perhaps harder to form an image of, but the cosmic clockmaker of the Deists may be close to it.

The difficulty arises when we put conceptions together which do not "fit," e.g., a personal passionless deity. Newman saw this as an image, but as one that cannot itself be conceived. It is inconceivable because when analyzed it results in a contradiction.

This analysis is a difficult one. Newman's own example of an inconceivable but imaginable entity may help some. He wrote: "The special property of the asymptotes may be an imagination. They may be true, but they are unintelligible. When true, they are said to be above reason, incomprehensible, mysterious.[31]" Now I suppose that it may be true that we can form an image of two lines which approach each other nearer and nearer and yet never meet, except at infinity (the latter phrase really meaning perhaps that they never meet). But I think it would be more appropriate to say that we have here a conception which cannot be imaged, rather than an imagination which cannot be conceived. Mystery would then involve a failure of our imagination, at least in a case like this. And it might also then be a failure of our imagination which makes a personal passionless God into a mystery for us.

One common response to this situation is "to remain open-minded in the face of mysteries, paradoxes, anomalies.[32]" This is Evan's description of Newman's attitude. The other response is the reaction of disbelief or rejection in the face of mystery, i.e., to assign a truth value of false to a mystery. I will argue later that these two quite different responses are in fact traceable to what Newman called the "personal" element in all human reasoning.

It now also becomes plain that one of Newman's persistent demands is a justifiable one. He urged that many of those who criticized religious belief made more rigorous demands on the religious believer than on others. It is true that many today are willing to be open-minded in the face of mathematical mysteries (e.g., a failure to be able to imagine asymptotes), and physical science's mysteries (e.g., to imagine how the universe could begin from a "big bang" and be expanding ever since in all directions, for into what then does the <u>universe</u> expand?) and yet become stubbornly close-minded when confronted with a religious mystery. This dichotomy of attitude was attacked by Newman, and justifiably so. This is not to suggest that Newman (or I) acquiesced in <u>any</u> so-called mystery or paradox. Newman demanded a rigorous assault on mystery by human reason. But he did not believe that because one came up against a mystery which did not yield to that assault one ought therefore claim that here irrationality or superstition (i.e., an easy credulity) and acceptance of (what I have called) one's failure of imagination.

I believe that this view of mystery as a failure of human imagination lies buried in much of Newman's analysis of religious epistemology. He tells us that because of the finitude of our minds we can only catch glimpses of God; we never see the Deity's wholeness or unity. We catch now this aspect, now that one. Those aspects may be incompatible with each other when we try to integrate them into a totality. But those aspects themselves are interpreted, analyzed, and understood by finite minds. In that process the aspects are not embodied wholly. Our reasoning about things or facts, as we have seen above, always reduces the richness of those things. The incompatibility of the aspects when reintegrated then may be due to our having misrepresented them in our analysis. Or it may lie in our inability to apprehend them adequately even with our most concrete intelligence. Or it may be a product of a failure of our imaginations being able to image those aspects together. Our mind in all of its operations—memory, imagination, implicit and explicit reasonings—is finite, and is thus a weak beacon projecting into the darkness of reality. Thus, not surprisingly, we are often confronted with mystery.

V

We began this chapter by raising questions about the use of terms like "mystery", and the "supernatural" in religious epistemology. What I have sought to do is to show that by using Newman's analysis of our intellect we can come to see these terms as appropriate and not as obscurantist. For Newman sought to show two things. The first was that "reasoning" is often too narrowly identified with a few certain processes of thought. To take reason to be coextensive with verbal reasoning, or methodologically pure and clear thinking, i.e., with explicit reason, is to misunderstand the nature of our rationality. Reason is a much broader base to our mental life than this.

Secondly, Newman tried to show that in any case no matter how "reason" was described, we are forced to recognize that human intelligence and all human mental activity are necessarily circumscribed in capacity. We are finite creatures, and that finitude limits our ability to see clearly the reality in which we live, and of which we are part. As Newman put it so well: only people who take their own conscience for God disbelieve mystery.

This means that we live our lives in ultimately mysterious reality. This mysteriousness is not found only in religious experience; twentieth century science also has discovered that our minds are finally unable to know reality fully. This is part of the force of our contemporary physics and cosmology.

So then to talk of mystery is to point to that which eludes our intellect, or that which is "above" reason, to use Newman's term. Mystery forces us to realize that there is more to reality than our natural minds can grasp; it leads us to see that there is something beyond our nature. There is then a genuine sense to "super-natural."

In our next chapter we will examine one particular set of situations in our reasonings in which we come up against that which ever eludes reason. Newman referred to those situations as the starting places of all reasoning, or the foundations of thought: they are the first principles upon which everything else depends. These are not knowable by reason; they too are "above" reason. By examining them we will develop further our understanding of what Newman meant by his claim that something might be "above" reason.

NOTES

1. Newman, John Henry. _Newman's University Sermons_ (London: SPCK, 1970), 8.

2. MacKinnon, D. M. "Introduction" in _Newman's University Sermons_, 20.

3. Newman. Op. cit., 262.

4. Newman, John Henry. _An Essay in Aid of a Grammar of Assent_ (Notre Dame: University of Notre Dame Press, 1979), 109.

5. Newman. _Ibid._, 90.

6. Newman. _University Sermons_, 257.

7. Newman. _Ibid._, 259.

8. Artz, J. "Newman as philosopher" in _International Philosophical Quarterly_ 16(S76), 274.

9. Shute, Graham. "Newman's 'Logic of the Heart'" in _Expository Times_ 78(May 67), 235.

10. Pascal, Blaise. _Pascal's Pensees_ (New York: E. P. Dutton & Company, Inc., 1958), 78.

11. Newman. _University Sermons_, 259.

12. Clifford, W. K. "The ethics of belief" in _Lectures and Essays, v. II_ (New York: Macmillan, 1879).

13. Newman. _Grammar_, 209.

14. On this see Gillian Evans' "Science and mathematics in Newman's thought" in _Downside Review_ 96(#325, October 78).

15. For discussions of this, see Ian Barbour's _Science and Religion_ (New York: Harper & Row, Publishers, 1968), and Thomas Kuhn's _The Structure of Scientific Revolutions_ (Chicago: The University of Chicago Press, 1970).

16. Newman. _Grammar_, 212.

17. Newman. _Ibid._, 281.

18. Newman. _Ibid._, 227.

19. Newman. _Ibid._, 281.

20. See note 4) above.

21. Reardon, M. G. "Newman and psychology of belief" in _Church Quarterly Review_ 158(July–September 1957), 317 and 324.

22. Newman, John Henry. _The Essential Newman_, edited by Vincent Blehl (New York: The New American Library of World Literature, Inc., 1963), 99.

23. Newman, John Henry. _An Essay on the Development of Christian Doctrine_ (Garden City: Doubleday & Company, Inc., 1960), 81.

24. Newman. _Grammar_, 114.

25. Newman, John Henry. _The Philosophical Notebook, v. II_ (New York: Humanities Press, 1970), 103.

26. Newman. _Grammar_, 55.

27. On this see the _Grammar_, 29.

28. Newman. _Grammar_, 38.

29. On this see the Grammar, 31.

30. Newman. _Grammar_, 56.

31. Newman. _The Philosophical Notebook_, 152.

32. Evans, op. cit., 251.

Chapter 2

I

In the first chapter, we found that Newman made a two-fold claim about mystery. He said that 1) mystery was reasonable, and that 2) our intelligence could to some extent illuminate that mystery. What we are seeking now is some particular evidence for these claims. So in this chapter we will investigate one intersection between our intelligence and the mystery in which we live. By focussing our attention carefully upon this intersection we will be able to make clearer what it means to say 1) that mystery is not ir-rational or anti-rational, and 2) that our reason can penetrate mystery and show up to some degree the order therein.

The intersection (or actually intersections) we will be reflecting upon Newman called "first principles." He often referred to these as antecedent considerations or antecedent probabilities[1]. Again, he called them presumptions, even prejudices, although when Newman used this latter term he meant nothing pejorative by it[2]. He used this sort of language in his work on this topic in the University Sermons.

In the Grammar Newman developed more fully his understanding of first principles. He wrote there that such principles are "the propositions with which we start in reasoning on any given subject-matter.[3]" He then proceeded to give several examples: the trust that we have in our powers of reasoning and memory; the proposition that there are things which exist external to us; propositions asserting that there is a true, a false, a right, a wrong, etc.

Newman did not always use the language of propositions when he wrote about first principles in the Grammar. In one place[4] he implied that an instinct could act as a first principle. This is an important insight on his part. I maintain that our experience of first principles (that with which we start in our reasoning on

25

a particular subject matter) is that they are often much vaguer than propositions. They may be pre-verbal, and are often unconscious.

To see this point more clearly, consider the following situations.

1) Rene Descartes decides to try to uncover something which is indubitable in order to erect a house of knowledge on a sure epistemological foundation. As a result of long careful reflection he comes up with the cogito. There have been many discussions since Descartes' time as to what the cogito is. Some believe that it is a proposition (i.e., an assertion) of some sort. Others see it as an argument. But when we really reflect upon it in a way similar to Descartes' suggested method in the Meditations, we come to see it more as an intuitive awareness of our own existential reality. "I am; I live; thinking is occurring of which I am immediately aware." The cogito reveals to me that what is nearest to (my) consciousness is my thinking and my being present to myself in that thinking. This is neither an argument nor a proposition so much as it is an intuition (rather like Newman's "instinct").

2) When we look at the face of a battered child, our response is immediate: horror, anger, grief. This response is built upon a realization that this is the consequence of evil. Yet the response occurs before we formulate any proposition about the existence and/or nature of evil.

3) We sit looking at a strangely shaped rock. Curious, we reach out to touch it and pick it up. Suddenly the rock moves, darting out of our reach. Startled, we may proclaim, "It's alive!" We here associate 1) "self-movement" with 2) "that which is alive," but we do this pre-verbally, nearly unconsciously.

What I am suggesting is that at least in some cases first principles are more like what Newman called implicit thinking or natural inference than like explicit or verbal reasoning. They are often intuitive approaches to our experience; again we might say that they are the points of view or the faces with which we open ourselves to experience. As such they can be pre-verbal, unconscious, virtually unrecognized. They are prejudices; that is, they exist prior to judgment about them. Thus Newman's less formal description of them in the University Sermons is at least as helpful to us as is the one in the Grammar. First principles may sometimes, and after reflection may usually, be formulated in propositions. But they are not always so. This is important because it shows up more clearly how much our first principles may live in the shadows of mystery. It makes clear how much of our conscious reasoning finds its roots in the unconscious, and thus shows us again that mystery is a pervasive phenomenon of our experience.

It could be argued that one important part of the work of the philosopher is to bring to light first principles. For example, the metaphysician seeks to reveal the first principles lying at the basis of world views. Now this work can be carried out in a variety of ways. For instance, conjecture, speculation, imagination, and fantasy, by producing new first principles, can lead to the creation of new world views. Or, working backward from a particular statement or perception, the metaphysician can be led to the revelation of the first principles underlying an already existing world view. Something like this is going on in the work of contemporary physics. Putting together a group of data, the cosmologist works back to what must have been the case if we are to account for the perceived data. We must not be naive about this, however. We have learned that the notion that there are wholly "raw data" is inaccurate; instead our observations too seem to be theory-laden—or in the terms being used here, whenever we perceive the world we bring to that perception our first principles. So the metaphysician must ever be careful to realize that any work (s)he does with observed data is already carrying some unexamined antecedent considerations.

To make this point clearer, consider this case: We see our hand moving while under the surface of the water. But something makes us suspicious about this visual perception. So we hypothesize that our hand is not moving. We wonder if it is the water that is moving and thus reflecting light rays in such a way that the impression is given that the hand is moving. To substantiate this hypothesis we reach toward the hand under water with our other hand. When we touch it, we receive no impression that the hand is moving; it feels motionless. To conclude that the hand is motionless on this basis is to accept (probably wholly unconsciously) that one sense (touch) is more trustworthy in this situation than another (sight).

Of course the first principle we have just elicited can itself come under investigation. In order to do this, however, we will end up assuming other first principles. One contemporary analysis of the line of argument I have adumbrating here has been given by Michael Polanyi in Personal Knowledge. Using his phrase, what I have been claiming is that there is always at work some tacit knowledge in any investigation. We can always turn around and try to examine the first principles we have been using, but in doing this we now have other first principles (or tacit knowledge) which we are not facing, and from which we begin. This is inescapable. And it means that our intelligence is fundamentally always operating out of what Newman and I would call mystery. That is, its roots in any particular piece of

27

analysis are themselves not only unexamined but unexaminable. For to dig down and look at these roots, we must reach forth from other roots not before us. Or as Newman put it: such an analysis is untied at both ends.

This at first seems to trap us in an ultimate irrationality. But on more careful reflection, we see that this is not the case. In fact, our antecedent considerations or presumptions can almost always be inspected. They can be investigated and found to be reasonable or not. Those which turn out to be supportable we accept--notice--precisely because we find them to be reasonable.

Another important characteristic of first principles is that there are unique principles presupposed in any line of investigation which we may choose to pursue. On this point Newman depended upon certain parts of the Nicomachean Ethics. This is not surprising; Aristotle saw clearly that every field of inquiry varies from any other field. It varies first of all in the demonstrative success it can produce. So Aristotle wrote:

> Our discussion will be adequate if it has as much clearness as the subject-matter admits of, for precision is not to be sought for alike in all discussions...We must be content, then, in speaking of such subjects and with such premisses to indicate the truth roughly and in outline, and in speaking about things which are only for the most part true and with premisses of the same kind to reach conclusions that are no better...it is the mark of an educated man to look for precision in each class of things just so far as the nature of the subject admits; it is evidently equally foolish to accept probable reasoning from a mathematician and to demand from a rhetorician scientific proofs[6].

But Newman also held that each field of inquiry has its own set of first principles. There may be some overlap of these from one particular field to another; thus some twentieth century biologists have sought to reveal an overlap of first principles between the sciences of biology and chemistry. But if Aristotle and Newman are correct, such an overlap is unlikely to be exhaustive. So while every field of investigation has first principles which are necessary to the pursuit of knowledge in that field, those first principles also are usually unique to that field.

This approach is helpful in understanding once more the limits of our understanding. Most human beings are most successful in coming to know and understand certain ranges of human experience, but not others. This can be accounted for in part by thinking about first principles. If someone has difficulty with mathematics, and cannot see into what is going on in mathematical investigations, one place to look for an explanation of this is in whether or not that person is able to see with the mathematician's eyes; i.e., can that person take over the first principles of the mathematician? To be able to use first principles in a field of inquiry is like being able to see the world from a particular point of view. If we cannot live into that point of view, we are not likely to be successful in that inquiry. This is one difficulty with much twentieth century cosmology, produced after the Einsteinian relativity revolution. Many cannot take over the first principles of that physics; to such a person when a modern physicist proposes that the universe may be shaped like the back of a saddle, such a proposal sounds like nonsense. But it may sound like nonsense precisely because the first principles which guide the subsequent reasoning here are themselves obscure to the one bemused by the claim.

II

We have now reached a point in the discussion where we can begin to see what Newman meant when he wrote that first principles are always personal. Not many of us, if any of us, are able to take all points of view on the world. We may be able to see the world as a musician, and/or a poet, and/or a chemist, and/or as an agnostic. The possibilities for combination are of course endless. And we vary in the numbers of points of view we can take over, and the degrees of success with which we take each over. This means that my way of seeing the world is surely different from the way in which any one else sees it. For instance, I am a trained zoologist, medical technician, philosopher, and theologian. I am also a father and teacher and counselor. The first principles that go along with these activities and pursuits I have more or less successfully taken over. They work in me when I am carrying on an investigation in particular ways. So when I am arguing about a moral dilemma, my thinking may be guided by theistic first principles. And when I seek an example in a philosophical argument, I often think of a biological situation which may be analogous. This sort of unique personal interaction between first principles is evident in Newman's case also. In several of his discussions about the relationship between religious faith and philosophical proof he used examples drawn from mathematics. Newman demonstrated an early interest in mathematics and physical science; while he never developed that interest very fully, still he apparently was able to operate with many of the relevant first principles. He could see the world, at least to some extent, as did the mathematician and the natural scientist.

Newman believed that first principles are always personal. He meant that since we are all unique individuals, with unique histories and combinations of experiences, our first principles, which reflect those histories and that experience, will be uniquely ours. This means in turn that we may have real difficulty in "trading" first principles, and in analyzing them together. Our experience is different; using Newman's view, that means that in turn our notions (developed out of our experience) will be different. Thus when we speak together (using words standing for notions and things) there will be dissonances all along the line. We will end up often talking at cross purposes; nowhere is this more likely to happen than when we are thinking together about our first principles.

In fact, this difficulty arises even in a discussion about the existence and nature of first principles qua first principles. One of the goals of some twentieth century philosophers (e.g., Husserl) has been to uncover a presuppositionless science. If Newman (and Polanyi) are correct, and I believe that they are, the search for such a science is hopeless. In fact, the urge toward a phenomenological uncovering of pure essences must be modified and become considerably more humble in its expected results. We cannot "bracket out" all presuppositions as we approach experience. Any essences uncovered will not be "pure," but rather necessarily will be viewed from some set of first principles.

On a view like the one presented here, a phenomenological investigation will be one which spends a good deal of time first of all bringing to light those first principles used by the investigator which are relevant to the field of inquiry in question. Those first principles will be studied in order to determine their reasonableness. Once this is done, (and this is itself a job to which one may have to return again and again, as Husserl suggested phenomenological investigation is likely to be), then one can turn to the field of inquiry to elicit essences.

There is an important consequence of this discovery that we use first principles in a unique way. Newman emphasized that since any field of inquiry has its own first principles, fields of inquiry are not open to any chance inquirer. As he wrote in the University Sermons, "What science...is not recondite in its principles? Which requires not special gifts of mind for its just formation?[7]" He would argue that in order to do a good job in a discipline, the investigator must grasp the first principles of that discipline. This suggests that someone who has not taken over the first principles of a discipline is also not going to be a fit investigator in that discipline.

A simple example here will illustrate and support this point. In teaching students to use a microscope, one sometimes runs across the student who simply cannot see what is there to be seen in the microscopic field. I do not mean that the light does not reach the student's eye, nor that the microscopic image fails to present to that student what is there. Trying to get the student to recognize the Amoeba or Paramecium which I can find quickly and easily there in the scope, I begin to realize that the student cannot recognize what is there before him/her. The scope is operating properly; the student's eye and nervous system are operating properly. What is lacking is the student's having taken over a set of first principles which organizes his/her visual impressions in this situation in such a way that (s)he can identify that under the microscope as a particular animalcule.

This is a crucial claim. What it suggests is that someone who has not taken over a set of first principles may be unable to recognize certain events in his or her experience. When X occurs, such a person either does not notice X at all, or mis-identifies X (i.e., perhaps does not recognize some of its characteristics, or places it into the context of the rest of his or her experience inappropriately).

III

We have reached a place in this argument which is particularly important for the field of inquiry which is the study of religious faith. Newman urged that like any other field of inquiry, those who investigated religious faith had to be able to take over the relevant first principles. For faith too "proceeds...on antecedent grounds...it trusts much to presumption.[8]" Faith depends on "the general state of his mind, the state of his convictions, feelings, tastes, and wishes.[9]"

The critic of faith may believe that Newman has here given away the game, for this claim is just what such a critic believes 1) to be true and 2) to be intellectually culpable. It is precisely the role of presumptions, feelings, tastes, and wishes in a person's faith which the critic finds to be so suspicious. But Newman has a rejoinder which is most important here: "unbelief, indeed, considers itself especially rational, or critical of evidence; but it criticizes the evidence of Religion, only because it does not like it, and really goes upon presumptions and prejudices as much as Faith does, only presumptions of an opposite nature.[10]" (I am taking "unbelief" here to refer to the agnostic as well as to the atheist.)

In other words, Newman believed that the critic of Faith does not share the first principles of the believer, and so finds unacceptable what the believer holds to be evidence. But there are two things to be noticed about this.

1) The critic is not presuppositionless. No one is. We cannot operate in any field of inquiry without presuppositions. Thus the critic cannot maintain that he or she is simply intellectually purer than the believer because (s)he is free of first principles. Once the critic recognizes this, (s)he may claim that his or her (the critic's) first principles are at least not feelings, tastes, or wishes; i.e., the critic can maintain that his or her first principles are more intellectually respectable than are the first principles of the believer. This would have to be argued for, and Newman would suggest that this must be done. He would say the same thing about the first principles of the believer; as I have suggested, Newman strongly believed that faith should be investigated by reason. He was not an obscurantist.

But Newman would suggest that in fact the critic's first principles also will be discovered to proceed from his or her feelings, tastes, and wishes. First principles are the products of, or find their roots in the personality, the uniqueness of the individuality of the person who holds them. That is, first principles proceed from who we are, as a whole person. They do not, and Newman would probably say, they cannot proceed from our intellects alone. Thus the critic will discover that his or her first principles have many of the same sources as do the believer's.

2) If the argument about first principles given above is correct, the critic may be unable to recognize as evidence for faith certain events or aspects of experience. That is, because the critic does not share the first principles of the believer, he or she may overlook at least some of what the believer finds to suppport his or her faith. Not being able to see reality with the eyes of the believer, the critic may not be able to notice what is there.

This is an enlightening realization. Here we have a classic case of persons talking past each other because they do not share first principles. And we can see why Newman wrote, "Never do we seem so illogical to others as when we are arguing under the continual influence of impressions to which they are insensible.[11]"

We have seen now that Newman held that faith proceeds from a particular set of first principles. He also tried to show how such first principles get taken over by a believer. Newman produced a variety of suggestions about how this occurred. These ranged from the theological to the psychological. The theological responses included the following.

In the University Sermons he wrote that "baptism (has) a power, at least of putting the mind into a capacity for receiving impressions.[12]" Newman thus apparently believed that a sacramental act could prepare a mind so that it became receptive to certain data. But Newman pointed to much less controversial methods for the taking over of religious first principles. So in the same place in the Sermons he pointed to "the habitual and devout perusal of Scripture...the gradual influence of intercourse with those who are in themselves in possession of the sacred ideas...the study of Dogmatic Theology...a continual round of devotion[13]." This approach reminds us of Pascal's advice: "You would like to attain faith...learn of those who have been bound like you...Follow the way by which they began; by acting as if they believed, taking the holy water, having masses said, etc.[14]"

This approach is one which has been strongly criticized. If it is read as suggesting that we stifle our doubts by numbing our intellects then it would appear to be a reprehensible suggestion. But neither Newman nor Pascal meant to suggest that we are to browbeat our intellects into submission before our feelings and wishes. Rather they meant to say that just as scientific reason has its method, which can be learned and improved upon by study and practice, so does the reason of faith. Much of a scientific education is repetitious. One learns some taxonomy in high school biology. One returns to taxonomy in the first college course in biology. Then there is vertebrate zoology: taxonomy is gone through again. And mammology: more taxonomy. Each time one goes through the same material, usually in increasing detail. Nonetheless, repetition here eventually leads to one seeing the biosphere taxonomically. This is of course only one example and one aspect of coming to see the world as a biologist. The reading of texts; the study of specimens; association with other biologists: all of this leads to one's taking over the first principles of biology. And for some persons, those first principles are gained quickly indeed. Their experience or their intuitions, perhaps their nature as well as their nurture, brings them quickly to the biologist's way of seeing the world.

This sort of process is what Newman means to point to as part of the way in which one takes on the first principles of the theist. It is not a matter of anesthetizing one's intellect; it is a matter of learning to recognize what is there.

Again notice the converse of this. The student who studies no taxonomy will not see the world in quite the same way as does the taxonomist. In fact, specific relationships between individuals are likely to go unnoticed by such a student. A similar thing is true in the case of the person who has no experience or training in theism. Some data are likely to go unnoticed by him or her too.

This discussion is acceptable as far as it goes. But Newman saw first principles as being tied to the person, and even personality in what I take to be an even stronger sense. As an epigram expressing this view of Newman's one might say that if one wants to understand who X is, then look to her or his first principles. That is, I am identifiable as the person I am by an examination and identification of those first principles which are mine. Or, my personhood is my set of first principles. Or, put most strongly, I am my first principles; my first principles are me.

This view can be found in Newman's later writing on this matter, especially in the _Grammar_ and in the _Philosophical Notebook_. So he wrote in the _Grammar_ that "all reasoning begins from premisses, and those premisses (arise)...in their elements from personal characteristics, in which men are in fact in essential and irremediable variance one with another.[15]" And, each of us "looks at the world in his own way...This is the case even as regards the senses...even when we agree together, it is not perhaps that we learn from one another, or fall under any law of agreement, but that our separate idiosyncracies happen to concur.[16]"

In developing this position Newman had recourse to what he called the "illative sense." He was not particularly lucid about this notion, but what he meant can be made somewhat clear by examining his discussion of what he held to be an analogous faculty, i.e., _phronesis_. Again Newman was thinking of Aristotle's work in ethics throughout this reflection. Newman wrote about _phronesis_:

> (Aristotle) calls the faculty which guides the mind in matters of conduct, by the name of _phronesis_, or judgment. This is the directing, controlling, and determining principle in such matters, personal and social. What it is to be virtuous, how we are to gain the just idea and standard of virtue, how we are to approximate in practice to our own standard, what is right and wrong in a particular case, for the answers...to these and similar questions, the philosopher refers to no code of laws...because no science of life, applicable to the case of an individual, has been or can be written...An ethical system

> may supply laws, general rules, guiding
> principles, a number of examples...but who is to
> apply them to a particular case? Whither can we
> go, except to the living intellect, our own, or
> another's?...The authoritative oracle...is seated
> in the mind of the individual...It comes of an
> acquired habit, though it has its first origin in
> nature itself[17]

I have quoted this passage at length because it will prove to be
one which helps us in getting a grasp of Newman's notion of the
illative sense.

Notice that the ultimate springs of phronesis lie "in nature
itself." Newman meant that my phronesis springs from who I am.
My faculty of judgment, or as we would more likely put it today,
my decision making proceeds from my unique individualness, from
the core which is my personhood. How I operate in the world as a
moral decision maker is determined by who I am.

Such decision making is the activity of what Newman here
calls a living intellect. Using the terminology developed in our
first chapter, we could say that it is the activity of a concrete
intelligence, or of implicit reason. Such an intellect always
occurs in a particular historical, social, personal context. In
twentieth century language, Newman here points to phronesis as an
existential category, or a lived experience. What he denied was
that phronesis could be seen as an abstracted intelligence.
Moral decisions are lived, are existential, and therefore are
always personal. One thinks of Sartre's emphasis on our being
necessarily forced to choose on our own terms, and out of our own
freedom. Newman would not go to Sartrean extremes on this, but
he would feel some sympathy for this emphasis in Sartre's
philosophy. There can be no completely adequate science of lived
moral dilemmas; when we face moral problems we face them
necessarily out of our personal centers. We face them from who
we are; we can only choose out of that center who we are. So no
universal description (no science) can be written here; universal
laws can not be developed which are compulsory, either morally,
psychologically, or ontologically.

There are of course difficulties with this view. Pushed to
a (Sartrean) extreme, morality seems to disappear before our
eyes. It is certainly correct that we are always in a sense
alone in making our moral choices. But to recognize that
phronesis arises primordially from nature is also to suspect the
possibility that human beings share something which allows for
some sort--however vague--of science here. This would suggest
further that if we agree together it may not be merely that "our
separate idiosyncracies happen to concur." Rather, our agreement

is able to tap here that shared natural source of our moral judgments.

Since the illative sense is a parallel faculty to phronesis, then Newman must have believed that much of the discussion and description of the latter faculty is applicable to the illative sense too. We will now develop that application.

Phronesis has the following three characteristics: 1) It is a directing, controlling, and determining principle used in a particular aspect of our existential life, i.e., moral dilemmas. 2) It is found in the mind of the unique individual, and is not an abstract intellect, or science of human behaviour, or transcendent code. 3) Its origin lies ultimately in the very nature of the person.

The illative sense will have similar attributes. The illative sense is the source of first principles, in particular those first principles having to do with reasoning. Phronesis guides our conduct; the illative sense directs, controls, and determines our reasoning. The illative sense acts when we accept or begin to reason from an assumption[18]. And it works throughout and includes the conclusion of the reasoning process, for as Newman wrote: "the Illative Sense, that is, the reasoning faculty...has its function in the beginning, middle, and end of all verbal discussion and inquiry, and in every step of the process.[19]"

Secondly, the illative sense is discoverable only in individuals. It is not some transcendental faculty, nor is it a transcendental ego. We can not examine the illative sense abstracted from its concrete embodiment in particular persons. Just as moral dilemmas arise in a particular time and place for particular persons, and moral conduct is then acted out by such persons making decisions guided by their personal phronesis, so problems which demand a thinking out or reasoning process arise in particular times and places for living individuals, persons, and must be worked on by the illative sense(s) of those persons.

Lastly, the illative sense finds its origin in the person whose sense it is. My reasoning process is mine, and no one else's. And of course no one else's illative sense is mine. In fact, we realize this in nearly every conversation we have with others. Think of Plato's Republic. The conversation related therein reveals the illative senses of the individual characters at work. Plato shows us that who one is influences how one reasons. Cephalus is an old man; his reasoning about justice proceeds from his experience, his present life-situation and his personal limitation. Then there is Thrasymachus. His thinking about justice too proceeds from personal assumptions (and underlying first principles). The way his thinking moves from those assumptions through an argument also is personal. His impatience, his arrogance, and perhaps his anxiety that he may not really have as good a grasp of the nature of justice as does Socrates all come through and influence his reasoning. Socrates' first principles and thus his illative sense also show through.

This is available to our purview in our own discussions with others also. We do not run across any completely abstracted, objective way of thought. Even contemporary logic shows that the axioms of a logical system must be chosen; there are no self-obvious axioms. And the reasons for choosing one set of axioms rather than another are guided by the purpose one is trying to achieve--a personal goal--and personal preferences, e.g., "elegance," "simplicity," "beauty."

There is in addition another important characteristic shared by phronesis and the illative sense. Newman pointed to this quality most succinctly when he wrote "(Phronesis) is a capacity sufficient for the occasion, deciding what ought to be done here and now, by this given person, under these given circumstances. It decides nothing hypothetical[20]." (Emphasis added.) Or, as he wrote about the illative sense, it enables the mind "to pass promptly from one set of facts to another, not only...without conscious media, but without conscious antecedents.[21]"

The emphasis on "nothing hypothetical" is important. The illative sense in involved in our ordinary reasoning; Newman associates it with natural inference [22]. Notions are not involved here; and this is reasoning done "unconsciously." We move here from facts to facts. Hypothetical matters, or abstract questions are not the focus of attention. This helps us to see further why Newman dissociates the illative sense from "science." Like phronesis, it is an existential category, and as such is concrete, not abstract.

Again, this analysis should not be pushed to an extreme. The illative sense is a source of first principles; since it is personal, our first principles are personal too. But if our earlier discussion is correct, we are able often to examine and reflect upon our first principles. That reflection leads to our uncovering what is reasonable about them. That reasonableness can be shared between us. This suggests in turn that our illative senses are not wholly dissimilar, or that they share certain qualities. They too, like phronesis, may have essentially common characteristics which are discoverable in each personal case. This commonality seems essential to account for our ability to reason together, especially about first principles. If this is correct, when we agree about first principles it is not just happenstance; rather we here come across instances of commonality between our illative senses.

In this chapter we have examined a particular intersection between our reason and the mystery in which we live, i.e., our first principles. We have seen that such first principles are presupposed in any investigation, and that in any study there are some such principles which are "behind" us, i.e., which are--in terms of <u>that</u> investigation--unexaminable.

We have also seen that such first principles are personal. Any one who reasons begins from a set of first principles which are personally his or hers. These principles proceed from our illative senses, and those senses are uniquely ours.

We have also seen that any field of inquiry presupposes a particular set of first principles. So when one reflects upon religion or religious experience, one brings to that study a particular set of first principles, e.g., theistic or agnostic first principles. Because first principles guide us as we perceive the world, what data are even recognized, and which data are seen as relevant are determined to some extent by our first principles. In our next chapter we will try to uncover what data the theist sees as relevant to his or her world view, and how (s)he constructs an edifice of evidence for his or her religious claims and religious faith.

NOTES

1. Newman, John Henry. <u>Newman's</u> <u>University</u> <u>Sermons</u> (London: SPCK, 1970), 187, 189.

2. Newman. Op. cit., 222, 230.

3. Newman, John Henry. <u>An</u> <u>Essay</u> <u>in</u> <u>Aid</u> <u>of</u> <u>a</u> <u>Grammar</u> <u>of</u> <u>Assent</u> (Notre Dame: University of Notre Dame, 1979), 66.

4. Newman. <u>Grammar</u>, 67.

5. Polanyi, Michael. <u>Personal</u> <u>Knowledge</u> (New York: Harper & Row, Publishers, 1964), especially Parts Two and Three.

6. Aristotle. <u>Nicomachean</u> <u>Ethics</u>, Book I, Chapter 3; W. D. Ross translation in <u>The</u> <u>Basic</u> <u>Works</u> <u>of</u> <u>Aristotle</u>, Richard Mc Keon, editor (New York: Random House, Inc., 1941), 936.

7. Newman. <u>University</u> <u>Sermons</u>, 327.

8. Newman. <u>Ibid</u>., 222.

9. Newman. <u>Ibid</u>., 226.

10. Newman. <u>Ibid</u>., 230.

11. Newman. <u>Ibid</u>., 334-335.

12. Newman. <u>Ibid</u>., 333.

13. Newman. <u>Ibid</u>.

14. Pascal, Blaise. <u>Pascal's</u> <u>Pensees</u> (New York: E. P. Dutton & Company, Inc., 1958), 68.

15. Newman. <u>Grammar</u>, 283.

16. Newman. <u>Ibid</u>., 291f.

17. Newman. <u>Ibid</u>., 277f.

18. Newman. <u>Ibid</u>., 297.

19. Newman. <u>Ibid</u>., 283.

20. Newman. *Ibid.*,   278.

21. Newman. *Ibid.*,   262.

22. On this see the *Grammar*, 260–261.

Chapter 3

I

Newman's Philosophical Notebook is a collection of notes
written over a period of several years, and not intended for
publication[1]. Still, the Notebook contains many seminal ideas,
and I have used some of these for our reflections throughout the
earlier chapters. In the Notebook is also found an image which
provides a benchmark for our work in this chapter. In March of
1861 Newman wrote:

> I consider that the proof for Religion is like a
> geometrical staircase, vaulted roof with
> pendants, etc. I mean where far more is done
> mechanically than seems possible, the artifice
> being hid. Each part depends on each other and
> the weight is thrown about on supports in a
> hundred directions.[2]

Newman reported that he had been influenced by Joseph
Butler's work in The Analogy of Religion. In particular, Newman
shared with Butler the notion that in the case of religion
relevant evidence supports the probable correctness of religious
assertions. This claim is meant to be in contrast to another
which sees "proof" in a stronger sense. On Newman's and Butler's
view a strict proof is not available for religious claims. For
them, Euclidean geometry and deductive logic are not appropriate
models when one approaches religious thought. One way to begin
to show that this is true is to return to our earlier discussion
of first principles. Euclidean geometry and Christianity both
have first principles (one might call these axioms), but the
axioms of Euclidean geometry appear to be more obvious than the
axioms (if we may appropriately use this term for the first
principles of religion) of Christianity. That the shortest
distance between two points is a straight line certainly seems
more patent than any first principles of Christianity (say, that

there is a force for good in the universe). Of course the notion of intuitive obviousness may be none too clear even in the case of geometry; the point here is merely that it is clearer in this case than in the case of religion. Thus at the very beginning of our examination--at the level of first principles-- we come upon a difference between religion and another field of thought and discourse.

In fact, not much of human thought lends itself to "strict proof." Science itself in all of its many garbs--physical, biological, social--is hardly capable of "strict proof" in a sense correlative with what that means in mathematics and logic. There are not only two alternatives in human thought--strict proof and no proof at all. What Newman argued was that because religion did not admit of strict proof, it does not follow that thereby it is to be written off as mere opinion or conjecture or superstition. Rather, religion belongs to that vast realm of human experience which while not strictly demonstrable, nevertheless is supportable by evidence and careful reflection and study. How it is supportable is the focus of attention in this chapter.

It must be recognized that on Newman's (and my) view the evidence we examine in the case of religion itself is ambiguous. No obvious way to understand that evidence reveals itself to us. It is because this is the case 1) that there is an argument needed and 2) that an argument is possible. We do not and need not argue that two plus two equals four. To grander questions, broader questions, existential questions, questions of meaning, there are no obvious answers. Thus argument in the sense of disagreement may well be inevitable and frequently even insoluble. What we seek in such situations is the most likely solution. To do this we can ask a series of questions: which is the least convincing reply? Which reply covers the most of the evidence? Which reply is the least arbitrary? To answer such questions in turn, we must come up with two things. First of all, we need criteria to assess the proposed solutions. That is, if we are to try to decide, e.g., which is the least arbitrary response, we must understand what is involved in arbitrariness, and one way to do this is to come up with a set of criteria which picks out more arbitrary responses from less arbitrary ones.

But secondly, there must be a framework within which to place these criteria. That is, anytime we develop such criteria they must occur within a larger interpretive schema. The criteria themselves derive their significance from a framework, a way of understanding significance and insignificance. Thus there are several levels to the construction of a "probable proof." Our task now is to begin to make plainer what is meant by a "probable proof."

Basil Mitchell in The Justification of Religious Belief uses an image of what a probable proof must not be taken to be. Says Mitchell, a probable proof is not a series of buckets set inside each other, each of which is leaky. That is, putting one leaky bucket inside of another leaky bucket, and then another inside of those, etc., etc., is not to construct a probable proof. A whole series of telescoped leaky buckets still leaves you with leaky buckets, and that is all[3].

Now in a sense this is accurate. We need to be clear about just what is meant by a "leaky bucket" however. A piece of evidence which can be understood in several ways is not a "leaky bucket." Rather, when such pieces of evidence are put together in one particular way they make more sense than when they are put together in some other way. The process of eliciting and showing this more reasonable way of understanding the evidence constitutes (as I understand it) the making of a probable proof. The mere fact that a piece of evidence can be viewed in more than one way does not make that piece of evidence insignificant (or even a negative factor) in the development of a probable proof.

Leaky buckets arise in situations when there are strong convincing arguments against seeing a piece of evidence in a particular way. Or to say this another way, a leaky bucket is present when there are other ways of understanding the evidence which make a good deal more sense than the one which we are calling a leaky bucket understanding. It is the seeing, the understanding, the interpretation of a piece of evidence which is a leaky bucket.

Mitchell's point is important. A probable proof must not be taken as a collection of weak improbable arguments strung together in the hope that they mislead or overwhelm our intellect. As Newman's image quoted at the beginning of this chapter displays, a probable argument is one in which each piece does work, and where each piece has some important strength of its own; it is just that no one piece can carry all of the weight by itself. To accomplish this task, other pieces are necessary; the work is finally accomplished together by individual pieces all of which contribute in a positive way, and all of which are valuable in their own right.

In the University Sermons Newman wrote "conviction for the most part follows, not upon any one great and decisive proof or token of the point in debate, but upon a number of very minute circumstances together[4]." As Artz rightly says about Newman's view:

> Certitude...does not grow by mere addition of
> probabilities, but by their cumulation and
> convergence. 'Cumulation' means their relation
> to each other, how they support, correct,
> complete, confirm each other, <u>especially if they
> result from different spheres of experience</u>...it
> is rather the question of a multiplication than
> of an addition. 'Convergence' means that in this
> manner of mutual support and confirmation they
> approximate the weight of a correctly formulated
> proof. They converge toward this proof as their
> limit.[5]

These suggestions demand some clarification. A probable
proof may work in several ways, and at different levels. Such a
proof gathers together "circumstances." Circumstances here may
refer to events, thoughts, understandings. Newman uses as
examples of such a proof the impressions that this person seeks
some particular goal, or that that person is unhappy. He says
that we get impressions about such things from a variety of
circumstances: "much depends...on manner, voice, accent, words
uttered, silence instead of words, and all the many subtle
symptoms which are felt by the mind...This...is...what is called
a moral proof[6]."

At this level a probable proof gathers together a variety of
(barely) noticed data, from a variety of spheres of experience.
Past history with the person (memory); experience with others in
a similar situation; projection of oneself into his/her place;
and undoubtedly many more sorts of data play a role in our
arriving at (completing a probable proof of) our conclusion.

Another way to say this is to say that a probable proof
draws out threads of relation; it points to articulations which
are puzzling, and then seeks to make available a reasonable way
to understand such relationships. Now there are two tests of the
adequacy and appropriateness of such a proof and its conclusion.
First of all, they ought to gather together in a <u>coherent</u> way
those circumstances which are being studied. Notice here that
again a prior first principle is at work. To discuss a proof of
any sort, but in particular to discuss a probable proof, one must
assume that coherence is a reasonable expectation. That is, 1)
one begins here with the impression that these circumstances need
to be explained, and 2) with the expectation that these
circumstances are explicable, that they <u>can</u> be made sense of. If
one denies this, if such circumstances are taken to be surds,
unreasonable, inexplicable givens, then one fundamental
motivation for developing a proof of any sort is undercut. This
seems to be similar to a view of Bertrand Russell. He argued
that at least some circumstances (say, the existence of a <u>uni-</u>

verse) need no explanation; they just are. When one sets out to construct a probable proof (a coherent understanding of such circumstances), the starting point is quite different. One comes across circumstances which cry out (to this person) for explanation. This puts into motion the work involved in developing a probable proof of a particular interpretation of those circumstances. But that is a journey on which a Russell will not set out.

So if one does begin to seek to develop a probable proof, then one must first of all come up with an understanding which will pull the various available relevant data together. Any circumstances which are relevant (appear to be related) can not be ignored, unless a reasonable basis is provided for eliminating them.

But secondly, a probable proof goes beyond this task of "gathering together." It points to other circumstances heretofore unnoticed, or at least heretofore not noticed as related to the circumstances being studied. These two aspects of a probable proof remind me of the work of a contemporary of Newman's, William Whewell. To elucidate further how a probable proof works, we will look briefly at Whewell's work. That work, arising in another discipline--philosophy of science--is helpful in further elaborating the activity of human mentality in assessing evidence.

Whewell worked as a historian and philosopher of science. His is in part one version of what in the twentieth-century has been called the hypothetico-deductive understanding of scientific method. That view sees science as a method of forming hypotheses and then deducing what events ought to be like if those hypotheses are correct; this is not widely accepted any longer as a fully adequate understanding of how science operates. Still, it is not an entirely inadequate view either, at least for much of the day to day work of "normal science" as Kuhn calls it.

Whewell's study is interesting here because he developed a notion of how evidence gets understood in scientific investigation which is similar to Newman's understanding of the development of a probable proof in religion. Whewell saw scientific investigation as involving at an early stage a colligation of facts. According to Whewell, the early development of scientific understanding involves two components: facts and conceptions. We will first examine what he means by this claim.

For Whewell, "facts" is not a self-evident term in and of itself. He believed that when we come across facts we experience them as the product of two events. From our standpoint, one of these is passive: e.g., our senses are affected by some stimulus. For example, light enters the eyeball and strikes the retina, after having been reflected from some object. The other event is an active one: our mind is active in all that we perceive or experience. We see a curved line; we can explain that in terms of light rays, etc., but that will not exhaust the "fact" that we experience. For we experience the line as convex or as concave, and the experience of that fact (a concave line) involves an act of the mind. To put this in contemporary language, all observation is theory laden. Thus at the very beginning of the development of scientific understanding, we begin with a theoretical component. To return to Newman's language, Whewell too realized that we always begin with first principles.

For facts to be made sense of, they must be referred to conceptions. Whewell drew a distinction between Ideas and conceptions. Ideas he held to be

> certain comprehensive forms of thought,--as space, number, cause, composition, resemblance...(Conceptions are) special modifications of these ideas which are exemplified in particular facts...a circle, a square number, an accelerating force, a neutral combination of elements, a genus[7].

The growth of scientific understanding involves a dialectic between facts and conceptions. That is, facts are referred to conceptions, and then conceptions are referred back to and tested against facts. Not only is observation theory-laden on this view, theory is tested against fact. Scientific labor involves the constant interaction of these two.

When facts are bound together by conceptions, eventually general propositions--the very stuff of scientific thought--arise. This is the process Whewell called the colligation of facts. Whewell wrote: "we may apply this term to every case in which, by an act of the intellect, we establish a precise connexion among the phenomena which are presented to our senses[8]." This Whewellian process, which Whewell holds to be an important aspect of the development of scientific understanding, looks to me to be markedly similar to what Newman believed goes on in religious thought.

After the colligation of facts has occurred, the scientist finds him- or herself in possession of a general proposition--a hypothesis. This hypothesis must now be tested to determine its adequacy. Whewell proposed that to do this the scientist used three criteria: the ability of the hypothesis adequately to explain all the relevant facts, the capacity of the hypothesis to foretell facts not yet observed, and the ability of the hypothesis to explain and foretell facts of a different kind from those used initially to formulate the hypothesis. This last process involves what Whewell called a consilience of inductions[9]. It is to this second aspect of his investigation of scientific method that we will now pay some close attention.

Whewell held that the reasonableness of a hypothesis is supported by our ability to predict correctly facts of the same sort as those which led to our producing the hypothesis in the first place. But more significant evidence is supplied to support our hypothesis if we can explain and predict facts of a different sort. For no

> accident could give rise to such an extraordinary coincidence. No false supposition could, after being adjusted to one class of phenomena, exactly represent a different class, when the agreement was unforeseen and uncontemplated. That rules springing from remote and unconnected quarters should thus leap to the same point, can only arise from that being the point where truth resides[10].

Whewell believed that this positive evidence of the correctness of our hypothesis is strongest when it allows us to draw together some other hypothesis or hypotheses under a broader principle. To show what he means, here is one of Whewell's own examples from the history of science:

> it was found by Newton that the doctrine of the attraction of the Sun varying according to the Inverse Square of this distance, which explained Kepler's Third Law of the proportionality of the cubes of the distances to the squares of the periodic times of the planets, explained also his First and Second Laws of the elliptical motion of each planet; although no connexion of these laws had been visible before.[11]

Whewell believed that there was no example from the whole of history of science in which a consilience of inductions had occurred, and yet the hypothesis which drew other hypotheses together under itself had later proven to be in error.

This process of the consilience of inductions also leads to a gradual simplification of scientific explanation. What Whewell means by this is that "new suppositions resolve themselves into the old ones, or at least require only some easy modification of the hypothesis first assumed: the system becomes more coherent as it is further extended[12]." In other words, if our scientific work is proceeding properly we do not end up with epicycles.

III

This has been a long aside. We began by looking at some preliminary suggestions from Newman about the nature of a probable proof in religion. Certain hints in that discussion reminded me of Whewell's work. So we have briefly examined what Whewell had to say about how scientific explanation is developed. My task now is to show the relevance of that discussion to Newman's understanding of how religious explanation is developed. One outcome of this section will be to show that there are not rigid disparities between the operations of human reason in science and in religion, but rather strong similarities. The dialogue between science and religion need not be one of disagreement and rejection, but one of cooperation and accord.

Newman's comments on "probable proofs" are scattered throughout his work. We saw earlier that in the University Sermons he talked about a "moral proof" (see page 43 above). I am holding this term to be the equivalent of what he elsewhere calls a "probable proof".

We can begin to see that Newman's view of a probable proof is similar to Whewell's view of scientific investigation by examining a series of Newman's reflections on this point. For instance, in An Essay on the Development of Christian Doctrine Newman wrote

> these doctrines are members of one family, and suggestive, or correlative, or confirmatory, or illustrative of each other. One furnishes evidence to another, and all to each of them; if this is proved, that becomes probable; if this and that are both probable, but for different reasons, each adds to the other in its own probability[13].

If we take "doctrines" here to be something like "hypotheses" in Whewell's language, we find a group of hypotheses providing mutual support for each other. This is a preliminary movement in a salience of hypotheses, or a consilience of inductions. Newman expressed similar ideas elsewhere:

> My argument is in outline as follows: ...that certitude which we were able to possess, whether

48

> as to the truths of natural theology, or as to
> the fact of a revelation, was the result of an
> assemblage of concurring and converging
> possibilities.[14]

And perhaps most remarkable is this argument from the Grammar:

> physical Astronomy and Revelation stand on the
> same footing. Vince, in his treatise on
> Astronomy...after speaking of the proofs of the
> earth's rotatory motion...says, 'When these
> reasons, all upon different principles, are
> considered, they amount to a proof of the earth's
> rotation...which is as satisfactory to the mind
> as the most direct demonstration could
> be'...Compare with this avowal the language of
> Butler...'Probable proofs,' he says, 'by being
> added, not only increase the evidence, but
> multiply it. The truth of our religion...is to
> be judged by the whole evidence taken
> together'...Here, as in Astronomy, is the same
> absence of demonstration of the thesis, the same
> cumulating and converging indications of it, the
> same indirectness in the proof...It is by the
> strength, variety, or multiplicity of premises,
> which are only probable...by objections overcome,
> by adverse theories neutralized, by difficulties
> gradually clearing up, by exceptions proving the
> rule, by unlooked-for correlations found with
> received truths...by all these ways...it is that
> the practised and experienced mind is able to
> make a sure divination that a conclusion is
> inevitable[15].

I have quoted this last passage so extensively because it is
as good a description as one can find in Newman's work of his
view of the development of a probable proof. In addition, it
shows up several similarities in that view and the view of
Whewell. Thus, we will use it to guide our reflections in much
of the rest of this chapter.

One way to think about Christian doctrines is to see them as
hypotheses about the nature of reality. They are more than this,
no doubt; but one intelligible interpretation of them is to say
that they attempt to tell us something about how the world is,
and how it operates. (There are persons who would deny this, but
I believe that they fail to understand what many religious
believers seek to do when they make religious statements. I
believe that when such believers make religious claims they are
trying to tell us about reality; they are not, for example,

49

simply making aesthetic or moral recommendations.) In this sense, such doctrines share certain features of scientific hypotheses. In particular, they attempt to construct a unitary vision of reality, just as Newtonian theories attempt to construct a unitary vision of reality. That is why Newman calls Christian doctrines "members of one family;" they are related to each other, and reflect each others' features. In this way, while this doctrine may relate primarily to one aspect of human experience, and that doctrine relates primarily to some other aspect, taken together these doctrines attempt to draw all of human experience within the field of one explanatory vision.

It may be important to note here that some have argued that science describes and does not explain at all, whereas one primary difference between religion and science lies in religion's compulsion to explain. I believe that this distinction is an important one to notice and pay attention to. But ultimately I think it oversimplifies both disciplines' tasks. Science often seems to suggest that to know how is to know why (to describe accurately is to explain). And science also recognizes that there are questions of explanation which demand responses: it just holds that often its methods do not permit the resolution of such issues. Again, religion is certainly not uninterested in the "how" questions which trouble us; while sometimes it may answer such queries differently than does science, religion can also accept scientific theories and make use of them in its attempt to understand. Newman provides an excellent example of a theologian unthreatened by scientific investigation. In the Philosophical Notebook he has a remarkable passage in which he reflects upon Darwin's theory and finds it fascinating and reasonable[16]. So when I talk about explanatory visions as being one product of both science and religion, I recognize the complexity and to some extent ambiguity of that phrase. I do not believe however that we need to nor can make perfectly clear distinctions about what such a phrase may mean in either science or religion. The attempt to grapple in a reasonable manner with reality in both disciplines involves looking at both description and explanation (how and why), and that attempt is to what I am referring when I talk about a unitary vision of reality.

Newman recognized that Christian doctrines work together in a complex manner. Evidence for the accuracy of one doctrine may come from one field of human experience while evidence for another doctrine may not be found there at all, but lies in some other field. Thus, it may not be the case that a single doctrine is supported by the same evidence as another doctrine; nonetheless two doctrines supported by evidence (reasons) from different directions can still work together, and produce together another hypothesis supported by all of the evidence supporting the individual hypotheses.

That this is hardly unique to religion is not hard to show. The history of the development of evolutionary theory is replete with the formation of hypotheses in quite different realms of nature. Over the course of a century or two, geology, paleontology, anthropology, genetics, ecology, and ethology have each developed hypotheses which work together to support a theory of evolution. That theory, while not particularly convincing perhaps on the basis of the work in any one of those fields of investigation bcomes highly probable when they are taken together.

Newman helps us here again, for he provided a perspicacious image for understanding how human reason operates in such cases. He wrote in the Grammar:

> a regular polygon, inscribed in a circle, its sides being continually diminished, tends to become that circle, as its limit...In like manner, the conclusion in a real or concrete question is foreseen and predicted rather than actually attained; foreseen in the number and direction of accumulated premisses, which all converge to it...yet do not touch it logically[17].

The whole notion of convergence appears and reappears throughout Newman's discussion of probable proofs. Convergence is an approach to a limit: it is many lines of argument (reasoning) working together and pointing in the same direction. When this line of reasoning is put in apposition to that (perhaps heretofore held to be unrelated) line of reasoning, our minds are (inevitably?) drawn toward...we may be unclear about the absolute configuration of the endpoint, but its figure can be "foreseen" as Newman puts it, or foreshadowed, as I prefer to say.

It is important to note that the psychological mark of such a proof is held by Vince to be its being "satisfactory to the mind." That is of course a vague criterion (although one mentioned by others too: think of what William James wrote about the "Sentiment of Rationality"). Many a naif is "satisfactory in his or her mind" about propositions upon which we could easily throw doubt. And it might be held that the fanatic is "satisfactory in his or her mind" when in fact there is good reason to be quite uneasy with what that person holds to be true.

So, that a psychological criterion is proposed here at all may make us quite uncomfortable. But I believe that Vince and Newman (and James) are correct on this view. Ultimately, what we have to go on as the test of the appositeness of our beliefs is their being "satisfactory" to us. Now, let us agree, what counts as satisfactory to me may be quite different from what will satisfy you. Newman recognized this: remember that, as we saw above, his view of the whole reasoning process (including its outcome) was that it is _personal_ throughout. This means that we may well disagree about what is a satisfactory proof. Newman gave a clear example of this in the _University Sermons:_ "A good and a bad man will think very different things probable.[18]" This is just what provides the discomfort though. How are we to assess the correctness and/or adequacy of the probabilities held by different persons, if all we have to go on is the "satisfactoriness" of those probabilities to the individual minds?

In a sense, we have arrived at a parting of the ways. Those who demand that all proofs be as adequate as a direct demonstration will be uncomfortable with anything less than this, and may reject anything less as not being reasonable at all. They may hold that to suggest one has "reasonable" support for a belief can only properly mean that one has demonstrated it. Unless the proof is certain, these persons find more discomfort associated with acceding to it than with refraining from accepting it and thus remaining in doubt. W. K. Clifford again comes to mind here. On a view like Newman's, it would be important to examine the first principles of these persons, for it is at that level (i.e., of their first principles and of their illative sense) that we might be able to discover why they hold this view. That is, Newman would hold that it is in the individual personalities of these people that we must look for evidence of why they make their individual decisions about the acceptability or unacceptability of a probable proof. And I believe that Newman is correct here too.

Still, this may seem to throw us into an irrevocable epistemological relativism, and thus ultimately into ir- rationality. There is one clue provided which may allow us a way out of that. The "satisfactoriness" of a probable proof must have the quality of the satisfaction provided by the "most direct demonstration." Let us try to fill out this suggestion.

One criterion of the satisfactoriness of a direct demonstration (say a logical deduction) is that upon returning to it, one finds again that it works exactly as before. It is repeatedly successful in demonstrating its conclusion. Again, one may begin with the same premises, take different paths (perhaps longer or shorter than the path taken before), and end up (irrevocably--i.e., no matter which paths are taken) at the same conclusion. These two criteria (and there are probably others) are part of what make a direct demonstration so "satisfactory to the mind."

A probable proof may operate to produce a similar satisfaction in a similar way. That is, upon re-examining the converging lines of evidence in the way one studied them before, one's attention may again be drawn to the same conclusion. Or, one may re-order the way in which the evidence is brought together; one may draw closer two lines of evidence whose relationship was not examined with much attention before. One may attempt to draw into the net of one's relevant evidence data not used in a prior construction of the probable proof. If these tasks once more point in the same direction as before, the satisfactoriness of one's proof may approach that of a direct demonstration.

This also shows that the construction of a probable proof is no simple, blind labor. As Newman says, a great variety of lines of evidence are and must be used to construct a truly satisfactory probable proof: strong, varied, and multiple premisses; objections overcome; adverse theories neutralized; difficulties cleared up; exceptions proving the rule; unexpected correlations discovered. This is a long, careful process. Jumps to conclusions, unexamined assumptions, rejected adverse evidence: these moves (often made by the fanatic) play no part in the construction of a probable proof.

If one reviews this discussion of Newman's notion of probable proofs in religion and the earlier one about Whewell's notion of how scientific thought operates, one finds some striking similarities. Just as Whewell sees facts being made sense of when they are drawn together in the process he calls a colligation of facts, in a similar way Newman portrays various facts of religious experience being drawn together into a web of meaning.

But a closer similarity, and the one to which I want particularly to draw attention, lies in Newman's language of convergence and Whewell's discussion of the consilience of inductions. These two processes seem to me to be remarkably similar. A very similar back and forth interaction between hypotheses, together with a very similar directional development are present in these processes. Or to say this another way, hypotheses are tested alongside of and against each other, and in this process are drawn together toward a broadened, deepened understanding of our experience.

To make plainer the similarities between these processes, notice that Whewell believes that a consilience of inductions occurs when we are able to draw hypotheses together under a broader principle. Newman believes a similar thing occurs in religion; this is in part the force, I hold, of the image of the polygon inscribed in a circle (see above, page 50). What is happening here, in both instances, is a working together of hypotheses (in Whewell's language) or doctrines (in Newman's language). As this occurs, we think as follows: this hypothesis will explain these facts of experience, and that hypothesis will explain those facts. Can we draw these two hypotheses together in such a way that we can come up with one general principle which will allow us to understand all of these facts? If so, then we have a consilience of inductions; or, if so, then we have a convergence of doctrines. The point is, the same process of thinking is going on in both instances.

Perhaps someone could accept this much, and still hold that there is a major difference between how a scientist's thinking operates, and how the religious believer's thinking works. It might be held that the scientist deals with facts (e.g., the apparent movement of the sun across the heavens) which are much less assumption laden than are those which the believer studies (e.g., the apparent Real Presence in consecrated bread and wine). It may seem to be essential to be able to evaluate the facts of religious experience, and thence the individual doctrines which converge together in a theological understanding. Can these latter genuinely be held to be analogous with scientific hypotheses, or are such doctrines so different from those hypotheses that the parallel I have drawn is disanalogous because I am really comparing apples to oranges?

It is hard to know how to answer this question, either negatively or positively. To what can we appeal here as an "outside" criterion? That is, any answer proposed is likely to carry with it a presupposition that they are dissimilar, or that they are similar. For instance, consider the following two criteria which one might try to use to decide this issue.

One criterion might be to try to determine what the base of support is for scientific hypotheses, and what it is for religious doctrines. A rough measure of this might be how many people experience what believers count as facts to be explained, and how many people experience what scientists count as facts to be explained. This is at best a very rough criterion indeed, for I do not see how counting heads here could decide the <u>reliability</u> of someone's claiming to experience something <u>requiring</u> explanation. Consider the following example. Few people saw (or at least recognized that they saw) the world that Monet did; yet once he showed us that world (or got us to see that world), we too were able to recognize it. Now suppose someone looks at "Impression: Sunrise", and says, "I can't see what he sees". We are not inclined to say that this shows that Monet is wrong, but that this person fails to be able to perceive the world that Monet sees. We are not even inclined to judge Monet to be in error here, and the other person to be correct when we can not recognize Monet's world either. So whether or not someone experiences certain facts is not a deciding factor in determining the accuracy of someone else's perception.

But more significantly, this appeal to "how many other people experience what you claim to experience?" is often used in the modern Western world as a presupposition to determine the "scientific" appropriateness of facts to be investigated. It is not therefore an independent criterion (i.e., independent of the scientific point of view) to decide whether or not scientific hypotheses are analogous to religious doctrines.

A second criterion one might try to use here is a pragmatic one: i.e., one can ask about a hypothesis (or doctrine), does it work? Such a question however makes no sense in and of itself. Rather, we must provide a context in which to place the hypothesis to see if it works. In other words, we must ask does it work to this particular end, or in this particular context? I suggest that here we come upon another difficulty in comparing religious doctrines and scientific hypotheses. It is at least often the case that the context in which these different ways of understanding reality operate are dissimilar in important pragmatic ways. What the scientist is after (e.g., healing the physical disease of the physical body) is different from what the believer is after (e.g., making the person whole again). What I am suggesting is that again we have here no independent criterion which will allow us to decide if religious doctrines are really significantly analogous to scientific hypotheses.

If I am right so far, we have not been able to discover whether or not Newman's and Whewell's views are comparable in an important way. I believe that the solution to this problem lies at a different level than the one we have been examining. For those who insist on staying here, I would only say that if we have not been able to show that these views are comparable, neither has it been shown that they are not. This seems to me to be a good reason to look elsewhere for a resolution of this issue. So I would argue that the question is not whether religious doctrines are significantly enough like scientific hypotheses to make my analogy work. The question is whether or not Whewell's and Newman's descriptions of human reason's operation in, respectively, science and religion, in fact reveal to us a unitary phenomenon. That is, when we study Whewell's philosophy of science, and when we study Newman's philosophy of religion, are we led to see human reason at work in both science and religion in an importantly similar way? I believe that careful study of the arguments of Whewell and Newman reveals such

55

an important similarity. The significance of this study then is that if Whewell and Newman are correct about how we think (and I have tried to show that they are correct about this), and if their views are closely compatible, then we have shown that there are important similarities in human thinking which occur in a scientific point of view, and in a religious point of view. These are not separate compartments of human thought and experience. Science is not an isolated way to understand reality; neither is religion. Science and religion then (and ultimately I would argue, all human investigation and human attempts to satisfy the desire for understanding and meaning) proceed by similar routes. We have also seen with some clarity what those routes are: a consilience of inductions, or convergence.

IV

If what I have argued above is correct, we are then led to wonder just what attempts to understand reality from a religious viewpoint looks like specifically. That is, it is of interest at this point to see just how--concretely--religious understanding proceeds. What we are looking for here is how <u>convergence</u> operates: what does a consilience of inductions <u>look like in</u> religion?

I will provide only a preliminary answer to this question. This matter deserves an extended treatment in and of itself, and I do not plan to do this work at this point. Furthermore, what I suggest here is not meant to be definitive. That is, what I propose here is only <u>one</u> sketch of how convergence might operate to support a religious view of reality.

I suggest that religious doctrines often arise in the various ways about to be discussed. Then, doctrines arising in these different ways act together in the way that Newman suggests. No one doctrine, nor any one source of religious doctrine may be particularly impressive. But as they work together, as they press against each other, they together produce an edifice which makes a religious understanding persuasive.

a) The first source of religious doctrines is personal experience. Such experience has been extensively studied, perhaps nowhere more impressively than in the still classic <u>Varieties of Religious Experience</u> by William James. There are other documents: Paul's epistles in the New Testament; Muhammed's testimony in the Islamic tradition; what the prophets desribe in the Old Testament; the reports by Black Elk; the writings of John Wesley. (In order to show how these lines of evidence <u>converge</u>, I will use a particular example in each of these sections. Here let me point to what James finds to be present in all of these experiences: i.e., an "uneasiness" and its "solution."[19])

b) There is the phenomenon of revelation. What I am thinking of here is specifically what is held to be <u>authoritative</u> revelation. There are certain basic documents or persons against which (or perhaps better, in the context of which) religious doctrines are tested. the Torah; the Gospel of John; the Koran; the Rig Veda; the Tao Te Ching. Moses; Isaiah; Muhammed; Confucius; Jesus. Such documents, and the lives of these people, are <u>canons</u>, i.e., rules or guides for study and examination. It is possible of course to invest such canons with a sort of dead-hand weight; fundamentalists sometimes seem to move in this direction. If this is done, then "revealed truth" (whatever this means in a particular tradition) can stand in the way of better understanding. But at its best, revelation calls our attention to something not noticed before; at its best, its authoritativeness lies in its ability to get us to see more than we did before. (In this, revelation is similar to what an artist does; compare what I said about Monet earlier.) Thus revelation, operating through what <u>others</u> say or do or are (rather than through our <u>personal</u> experience, as in a)) also provides support for religious doctrines. As a relevant example here, think of the Old Testament prophet filling out the content of James' notion of "uneasiness" by crying "Let justice roll down like waters."

c) There is the history of religions. What I mean to point to under this heading are communities of belief: generations of generations which hand down teachings and interpretations of experience (i.e., religious doctrines). This works at several levels. I am not suggesting that merely because something is passed on from one generation to another that that makes it a credible support for a doctrine. (Although, I believe that this fact needs to be taken with some seriousness. Unless we are prepared to believe that earlier generations were obviously more credulous, gullible, or foolish than we are, we ought to pay serious attention to what they said about reality. Not to do so is to be guilty of temporal parochialism, i.e., the prejudice that our age is "advanced" compared to earlier ones. Perhaps we are in some ways; I believe though that we may well be less advanced than earlier ages in other ways, for instance in our ability to experience the transcendent. In any case, no obvious evaluation on this point is visible.)

What makes a history of doctrines significant is that in most religions there has been constant study, reflection, and testing of doctrines. There has been constant testing to see how <u>this</u> doctrine fits into a system of doctrines (cf. my "unitary view of reality"). Doctrines which have been seen not to fit into the system have either been rejected (cf. Docetism in Christianity), or have forced a revision in the system of beliefs (cf. slavery in Christianity). In this latter example, (which I am using in this section to go along with the earlier examples in order to reveal a "convergence") an uneasiness which occurs in the face of a perceived injustice associated with slavery is called to attention over generations of reflection and experience, and then is called to judgment (i.e., is changed). A religious world view has seldom been static, i.e., uninfluenced by new experience, and new understandings. Judaism (think of rabbinic schools); Christianity (think of the nearly <u>constant</u> historical arguments); Buddhism (study the documents and documents and documents); Islam (with its mullahs): all of these reflect historical communities of continuity and reflection.

d) The phenomenon of conscience plays a role here too. Our sense of something not being right or true; our guilt over what we have done; even our sense of relief upon repenting and being forgiven: all of these provide support too for religious doctrines. Newman has an insightful comment on this. He says in the <u>Apologia</u>, "if I am asked why I believe in God, I answer that it is because I believe in myself, for I feel it is impossible to believe in my own existence...without believing also in the existence of Him, who lives...in my conscience.[20]"

e) Lastly, there is also the evidence of natural theology. Human reason (in a narrow sense, say in the sense of explicit reason) also offers us evidence and arguments for religious doctrines. Arguments for the existence of God; arguements for the immortality of the soul; arguments about the meaning of omnipotence, omniscience, perfect Goodness, etc.: these contribute to a logical foundation-stone for the house of religious belief. Perhaps no one of these arguments is persuasive for anyone in and of itself. But together, and with the other lines of evidence we have just studied, these arguments add support for the probability of religious belief. In terms of my ongoing examples, we can think here of Kant, who argued for the intrinsic worth of every rational creature, thus contributing to a philosophical rejection of the acceptability of slavery.

Clearly, the lines of evidence which I have mentioned in these sections overlap. After all, one person's personal experience is another person's authoritative revelation. And revelation canonized becomes part of a historical tradition. We must also see that discussions in natural theology about omnipotence arise out of a historical community's tradition of referring to God as Almighty. This is all true of course. But the point is that if we study how some one person might support the probability of the appositeness of his or her religious

belief, those various lines of evidence would be just that--
various lines of evidence, for that one person. Thus a person
reflecting on the specific examples I have used in each of these
sections might very well be led by their combination to reject
slavery. I have already suggested that this sort of reasoning is
found in science too. Mendel's genetics; molecular biochemistry;
ethology: these are variations on a single theme in biology;
together they make up the symphony which is evolutionary theory.

I believe that the lines of evidence listed here (and I have
suggested that this list is by no means meant to be exhaustive)
do work together to provide probable proofs of religious claims.
Some lines may be better developed, more persuasive, even more
rigorous than others. But together they produce an accumulative,
converging, probable proof of which we must take account.

V

We have arrived at our journey's end. The preceding
chapters have led us to see that human reason can provide support
for religious assertions. But because reality is richer, deeper,
more profound, and more complex than our reason is able fully to
comprehend, we live in mystery. Part of that mystery is entered
into in the act of religious faith. Reason can make some sense
of our journey into mystery; to that extent it is to be honored,
and we ought to make diligent use of it. Reason must not however
be taken for a god, for that will only lead us astray. We are
finite, imperfect creatures; our understanding will remain finite
and imperfect. In the face of this truth, we can only be humble,
and recognize each other's first principles for what they are,
our attempts to bring cosmos out of the mystery in which we find
ourselves enveloped. We need not accept anything as reasonable;
but we need to recognize too that no one has infallibility in
determining just what is reasonable and what is not.

59

NOTES

1. Cameron, J. "John Henry Newman: Apostle of Common Sense?,"
The Second Cardinal Newman Lecture, October 24, 1982,
Manresa Educational Corporation, 6.

2. Newman, John Henry. The Philosophical Notebook, v. II
(New York: Humanities Press, 1970), 133.

3. Mitchell, Basil. The Justification of Religious Belief
(New York: Oxford University Press, 1981), 40ff.

4. Newman, John Henry. Newman's University Sermons (London:
SPCK, 1970), 274.

5. Artz, J. "Newman as philosopher" in International
Philosophical Quarterly 16(S 76), 274, emphasis added.

6. Newman. University Sermons, 274.

7. Whewell, William. The Philosophy of the Inductive Sciences,
v. II (London: Frank Cass & Company Ltd., 1967), 5f.

8. Whewell. Ibid., 36.

9. A good summary of all of this is found in C. J. Ducasse's
"Whewell's Philosophy of Scientific Discovery" in
The Philosophical Review 60(1951), 229f.

10. Whewell. Ibid., 65.

11. Ibid., 65f.

12. Ibid., 68.

13. Newman, John Henry. The Essential Newman, edited by
Vincent Blehl (New York: The New American Library of
World Literature, Inc., 1963), 134.

14. Newman, John Henry. Apologia pro Vita Sua (New York:
W. W. Norton & Company, Inc., 1968), 29.

15. Newman, John Henry. An Essay in Aid of a Grammar of Assent
(Notre Dame: University of Notre Dame Press, 1979),
252-254, emphasis added.

16. Newman. The Philosophical Notebook, v. II, 158.

17. Newman. Grammar, 253f.

18. Newman. University Sermons, 191.

19. James, William. The Varieties of Religious Experience
       (New York: Longmans, Green, and Company, 1902),507ff.

20. Newman. Apologia pro Vita Sua, 156.

INDEX

Jung, C.   5

Kingsley, C.   3

Language   10 ff., 17
Logic   6, 9 ff., 15, 41, 52, 58
Logique du coeur   6

MacKinnon, D. M.   6
Metaphysics   27
Method   6 ff., 11, 33, 50
Mitchell, b.   ix, 43
Moral   7, 35 ff.
Mystery   1, 12, 14 ff., 25, 27, 59

Natural inference   11 f., 37
Newman, J. H.
    Apologia   48, 58
    Essay on Development   15, 48
    Grammar of Assent   3, 12 f., 16 ff., 25, 34, 36 f., 49, 51
    Philosophical Notebooks   41, 50
    University Sermons   2 f., 25, 31 ff., 43, 52
    Tract 73   15
Notional propositions   18
Notions   17 ff., 30

Objectivity   9

Pascal, B.   5 f., 33
Personal knowledge   12, 29 ff., 32, 34 ff., 52
Phenomenology   30
Phronesis   34 ff.
Plato   36 f.
Polanyi, M.   27
Probable proof   ix f., 41, 43 ff., 48 ff., 59

Rationality   1 ff., 9 f., 21, 25
Reardon, M. G.   13
Reason   vii ff., 1 ff., 20 f., 25 f., 28, 35 f., 43, 46 f., 51 f.,
    55, 59
Religion   ix, 1 ff., 16, 41 ff., 48 ff., 54 ff.
Russell, B.   44 f.

Satisfactoriness to mind   49, 51 ff.
Science   9 f., 15 f., 21, 30, 33 ff., 42, 45 ff., 50, 53 ff., 59
Shute, G.   5 f.
Supernatural   1, 14, 21